THE ULTIMATE
BINGE-WATCHING
GUIDE

CHRIS ROBERTS

**CARLTON
BOOKS**

THIS IS A CARLTON BOOK

Published in 2014 by Carlton Books Limited
20 Mortimer Street
London W1T 3JW

Copyright © 2014 Carlton Books Limited

A CIP catalogue record for this book is available from the British Library.

ISBN 978-1-78097-644-0

Printed and bound by CPI Group (UK) Ltd, Croydon, CR0 4YY

Contents

A–Z Contents

Introduction

"No flipping!" – Larry Sanders.

Previously ... it was all about cinema. Yet the twenty-first century has increasingly seen many of us switch our preference to long-form TV, where the stories, characters and talent are now centred. From *The West Wing* to *The Thick Of It*, from *Hill Street Blues* to *True Detective*, from *Six Feet Under* to *The Walking Dead*, from *The Shield* to *The Bridge*, from *Friends* to *Girls* ... the television is being revolutionary.

You can go much deeper in (for example) a rich, rewarding 16-hour series than you can in a kiss-kiss-bang-bang blockbuster. The experience of watching an addictive, smartly-written, well-acted, top-level series is akin to immersing yourself in a book aimed at adults rather than dipping into a short story pitched at popcorn-munching kids. The stylised pictures come into your home, insistent on intimacy, forming a personal bond.

Creation and response are perhaps closer in sensibility to a Victorian serialised novel than the CGI-laden multiplex; at its finest the new TV is more Dickens/Trollope meets Scorsese/Altman than "Transformers Blow Up Hero-Man After A Car Chase". Extended suspense often comes as much through character as cliffhanger. Across a vast canvas, intertwining stories twist and shimmy and jack-knife to progress and obsess. Characters grow, shrink, dilate, reinflate. The three-arc structure becomes a 30-axis pyramid. And this paradigm shift helps the tales address the big issues of our time, whatever period costume is being worn.

We watch differently. No longer content to wait a week sitting through ads for the next episode, we buy, download or stream a series in its entirety and "binge-watch" in a few sittings, main-lining the adrenalized complexity.

Knowing the audience has elastic time to get to grips with its narrative, as opposed to a mere two hours in a movie, producers of these marathons can afford to carve characters as nuanced and contradictory as any human being.

Which is not to say we can't all enjoy a short, sharp, wickedly funny *Cheers* or *Family Guy* session now and again. Sometimes levity is the role of wit. Plenty of drama-steak in this book, but generous helpings of comedy-candy too.

Size isn't everything: the new generation of shows has pushed boundaries and broken taboos. (The 1970s is widely regarded as the peak of grown-up, articulate cinema, and that too didn't shy away from sex, drugs and the rebel music of its day.) From artful credit sequences to treated sound-beds, these visions offer an alternative reality, another world, where the viewer is invited to live, learn, laugh, cry, relate and escape; titillated, tantalised. And in an age of media fragmentation, for once we find ourselves all wanting to talk about the same thing around that mythical water-cooler...

In recent years, the award-winning, game-changing giants of the format – *The Sopranos, The Wire, Mad Men, Breaking Bad* – have been more chatted about, argued and tweeted about than any movie, with new shows constantly raising the bar. Comedy, too, has seen a golden age on both sides of the Atlantic, from *30 Rock* and *Modern Family* to *The Office* and *The Trip*. Fantasy and science fiction have broken fresh ground, from Joss Whedon's wit and wisdom in *Buffy the Vampire Slayer* to the dark, brooding heart of *Game of Thrones* or *Battlestar Galactica*. Inspired by the US front-runners, intriguing shows have emerged from the UK (*Sherlock, Luther*) and across Europe, with Scandinavia patenting a new genre of crime thriller. From Tony Soprano to Omar Little, from Saga Noren to President Bartlet, from Walter White and Jack Bauer to Carrie Mathison and Samantha Jones, we hail the multi-faceted heroes and villains who have demanded our loyalties.

The renaissance and easier accessibility has also

encouraged us to revisit old favourites in full – the influential classics and the vintage greats which have aged best are here too. It's not like TV began with HBO, it's just that HBO remembered how great it could be if you ignored family-friendly focus groups.

This book gathers and discusses 100 of the most important, resonant and outstanding TV box sets of recent decades (with no spoilers!) It might make you want to catch the shows you haven't yet seen and revisit the ones you have. The selection aspires to be an even-headed blend of universally acknowledged, popular landmarks and undervalued personal favourites. I accept that you can't ignore, say, *Doctor Who* or *Blackadder* – massive pop-culture monoliths even if I personally don't "get" them – but also feel it's somehow important not to let the likes of *Soap* or *NYPD Blue* languish in relative obscurity. *The Sopranos* or *Game of Thrones* don't really need anyone else championing them, but overlooked anti-crowdpleasers like *Nip/Tuck*, *Southland* and *Boss* just might. So it's the big hits and the near misses, and some food for debate.

Arguments were unavoidable: to appease the aggrieved, a list of nearly-made-its appears at the end of the hall-of-famers. (No power however could make me overcome my loathing of *The Inbetweeners* or *Utopia*, both of which have many fans, so there is a soupcon of subjectivity at play.)

TV being the most vibrant artistic medium of our time, hot new "buzz" shows (the macabre beauty of *Hannibal*, the rapid-fire zingers of *Brooklyn Nine-Nine*) will of course leap front and centre between my writing this and you reading it. We will be "so over" others. That only reaffirms the genre's vitality. Box sets will continue to think outside the box. Frank Lloyd Wright may have dismissed television as chewing gum for the eyes, but he was an architect, and didn't have cable. Tune in, turn on!

You may now flip…

Chris Roberts, London 2014

DOCTOR WHO

CREATED BY:	Sydney Newman, C.E. Webber, Donald Wilson
STARRING:	Matt Smith, David Tennant, Jenna Coleman, Billie Piper
DATES:	November 1963 – December 1989; March 2005 – present
SEASONS:	26 from 1963–1989, 7 from 2005 – present
EPISODES:	800 (97 missing)

SOUNDBITE:

"Do you want to come with me? If you do then I should warn you: you're going to see all sorts of things. Ghosts from the past, aliens from the future, the day the Earth died in a ball of flame. It won't be quiet, it won't be safe, and it won't be calm. But I'll tell you what it will be – the trip of a lifetime."

The Ninth Doctor (Christopher Eccleston)

REVIEW:

"It's family-friendly and adult-pleasing, over-the-top and nightmarish, witty and deep all at the same time."

Hollywood Reporter

The best British TV export of all time... and space?

Recognised as one of Britain's finest exports (as the longest-running, most broadcast science-fiction series in the world), *Doctor Who* has travelled a long, long way in space and time since emerging in 1963. His Tardis then was a blue police box. Now, the special effects are rather more dazzling and cutting-edge.

The show has a proud history of imaginative tales, fanned mythology and creative renewal, regenerating across the tenures of William Hartnett, Jon Pertwee and Tom Baker through to its 2005 revival via Christopher Eccleston and David Tennant. Most recently, in 2013, Matt Smith has passed the baton on to Peter Capaldi, the Twelfth Doctor. The Daleks, Cybermen and The Master are infamous adversaries.

A popular institution, *Doctor Who* has even prompted Steven Spielberg to say, "The world would be a poorer place without it." The modern-day trip, with labyrinthine plots, heavy symbolism and cute-but-independent companions, has become the BBC's flagship show, with hype and discussion reaching levels of hysteria. Ron Grainer's electronic theme music quivers in and a nation cowers behind the sofa, hooked on the hokum which Digital Spy called "the scariest TV show of all time". (They need to stay in more.) Sadly, 97 episodes were wiped or lost between '64 and '73, but there's more than enough for you to be carrying on with.

If you liked this you'll like:
Torchwood, Star Trek, Blake's 7.

STAR TREK

CREATED BY:	Gene Roddenberry
STARRING:	William Shatner, Leonard Nimoy, Deforrest Kelley
DATES:	September 1966 – June 1969
SEASONS:	3
EPISODES:	79

SOUNDBITE:

"Scotty, beam us up."
(Kirk never actually says, "Beam me up, Scotty.")
Captain James T Kirk

REVIEW:

"*Star Trek* was a very inconsistent show which at times sparkled with true ingenuity."
Rod Serling

Light years ahead of everything else on TV...

Now a seemingly limitless franchise of spin-offs, extensions, reinventions and blockbuster movies, it's easy to forget that the original, iconic *Star Trek* series only lasted three seasons and was cancelled for low ratings. Those three seasons are still repeated around the world, their kitsch and nostalgia factors countered by the undeniable presence of the seed of something prescient. "The City on the Edge of Forever" is generally acclaimed as its finest episode.

Space: the final frontier. The 1960s were obsessed with boldly going where no man had gone before, and for all the hokey plots and low-budget effects, *Star Trek* struck a chord with fans, who begged NBC to keep it going. Roddenberry's vision has since been vindicated, as the show has had a vast impact on popular culture, from stock characters to catchphrases. The *USS Enterprise* whisked around the Milky Way, sometime in the mid-twenty-third century, meeting aliens of all shapes and sizes and generally trying to do more good than harm. It was, of course, the lead characters who lent it longevity. William Shatner's Captain James T. Kirk, pompous, preening and – as Roddenberry put it – "Horatio Hornblower in space". The highly logical Commander Spock (Nimoy), half-Vulcan, all enigma. And Bones, Scotty, Uhura, Sulu and Chekhov: a righteous rainbow of ethnicities. (Less well known are guest appearances by Joan Collins and David Soul.) Warp speed ahead...

If you liked this you'll like:
Star Trek: The Next Generation, Deep Space Nine, Star Trek: Voyager.

MONTY PYTHON'S FLYING CIRCUS

CREATED BY:	Graham Chapman, John Cleese, Terry Gilliam, Eric Idle, Terry Jones, Michael Palin
STARRING:	As above
DATES:	October 1969–1974
SEASONS:	5
EPISODES:	62

SOUNDBITE:

"We interrupt this programme to annoy you and make things generally irritating."

BBC announcer

REVIEW:

"Their writing threw away the rulebook of traditional sketch writing, dispensing with punchlines and allowing sketches to blend into each other or simply stop abruptly. It was a technique already pioneered by Spike Milligan, but the ruthlessly self-critical Pythons mastered it."

BBC Online

"And now for something completely different..."

The dead parrot, the Spanish Inquisition, the Ministry of Silly Walks, Spam, "nudge-nudge" and "The Lumberjack Song" are part of the fabric of our popular culture now, though few would have predicted their impact and longevity as the 1960s became the 1970s. Surrealism, innuendo and "pythonesque" logic were pitched at the idiosyncratic mores of a rapidly evolving British society.

Mostly Oxbridge graduates, the intellectual yet wilfully daft Python team dropped in political and class references, name-checked philosophers, and adventured off into uncategorisable quasi-psychedelic tangents. Spike Milligan's *Q5* had debuted some months earlier, scrambling the conventions of television, and along with Peter Cook and Dudley Moore's shows, is thought by many to be the John The Baptist to the Python's very naughty Messiah. Cleese has said, "When we saw *Q5* we were very depressed because we thought it was what we wanted to do and Milligan was doing it brilliantly. But nobody really noticed *Q5*... the fact that Spike had gone there probably enabled us to go further than we otherwise would."

If you liked this you'll like:
The Hitchhiker's Guide To The Galaxy, Q9, The Mighty Boosh.

M*A*S*H

CREATED BY:	Larry Gelbart (adapted from the 1970 Robert Altman film)
STARRING:	Alan Alda, Mike Farrell, Loretta Swit, Jamie Farr
DATES:	September 1972 – February 1983
SEASONS:	11
EPISODES:	256

SOUNDBITE:

"War isn't Hell. War is war, and Hell is Hell. And of the two, war is a lot worse."

Hawkeye

REVIEW:

"In its initial season, *M*A*S*H* was in danger of being cancelled due to low ratings. Its final episode was a two-and-a-half-hour special which attracted the largest audience to ever view a single television programme episode."

tv.com

Tonic for the troops which resuscitated comedy

Robert Altman's satirical black comedy movie, starring Donald Sutherland and Elliott Gould, was an unlikely hit, depicting a medical unit (doctors and support staff) stationed at a Mobile Army Surgical Hospital during the Korean War. Its subtext, of course, was the Vietnam War, then ongoing, and it won an Oscar for Ring Lardner Jr.'s screenplay. When a shot at filming the original Richard Hooker book's sequel fell through, this TV spin-off came about. By the end of its eleven-year run, its finale "Goodbye, Farewell and Amen" drew a staggering 125 million viewers.

Fundamentally an oft-told tale of how laughter is the best medicine for adversity, $M^*A^*S^*H$ upped the stakes so that gallows humour was the antidote for bloodshed and horror. Many of the absurd stories were based on true recollections of real army surgeons, and could leap from farce to sobriety from one episode to the next. Wisecracking leads, such as "Hawkeye" (Alda), Klinger (Farr) and "Hotlips" (Swit) became as iconic as the "Suicide Is Painless" theme song. Hawkeye was considerably more liberal-leaning in the series than in the books, wherein he spoke of, "Kicking the bejesus out of the lefties just to stay in shape". Here, he was the smirking, waggish sage, declaring, "Insanity is just a state of mind".

If you liked this you'll like:
Cheers, Scrubs, Green Wing.

BARNEY MILLER

CREATED BY:	Danny Arnold, Theodore J. Flicker
STARRING:	Hal Linden, Max Gail, Steve Landesberg, Ron Glass
DATES:	January 1975 – May 1982
SEASONS:	8
EPISODES:	168

SOUNDBITE:

Dietrich: "Was that Mrs. Miller?"
Barney Miller: "Yeah."
Dietrich: "Past tense was unintentional."

REVIEW:

"The humour often plays on the multi-ethnic nature of the cast, with some stereotyping, but the writing evidences a mutual respect and co-operation, and shows sensitivity for the issues of the day."

Digitally Obsessed

New York's finest at their funniest...

The great 1970s cop/workplace sitcom. One-act episodes occur almost entirely within the detectives' squad room and Captain Miller's adjoining office in a run-down, beat-up, Greenwich Village police station. We rarely intrude upon their home lives. Instead, we get to know them through economical writing and deftly-acted scenes. Typically, complainants or suspects will drop in or be dragged in, giving different cops various sub-plots. Barney (Linden) tries to keep his composure despite the eccentricities of his staff and a mountain of bureaucracy.

At times the show is as dramatic as it is comedic, as developing narrative arcs (like Barney's frustration with red tape and his delayed promotion, Fish's ailments and reluctance to retire and Harris' desire to write a novel) could have easily been grafted on to *Hill Street Blues*. The credit sequence suggests a grimier New York. However, the charm of Linden and his ensemble made laughs inevitable, especially after Danny Arnold re-wrote scripts over and over. Taping the show in front of a live audience was dropped early on, as the actors were frequently waiting around for their lines until 2a.m. the night before. *The New York Times* has reported that many police officers cite this as the most realistic of all cop shows: most of the "action" hides off screen, and none of the cast are pin-ups – they just work hard and crack jokes.

If you liked this you'll like:
Soap, Taxi, Brooklyn Nine-Nine.

FAWLTY TOWERS

CREATED BY:	John Cleese, Connie Booth
STARRING:	John Cleese, Prunella Scales, Andrew Sachs, Connie Booth
DATES:	September 1975 – October 1979
SEASONS:	2
EPISODES:	12

SOUNDBITE:

"You'll have to forgive him. He's from Barcelona."

Basil Fawlty

REVIEW:

"Long John Short On Jokes."

Daily Mirror, from a review of the first episode.

The hotelier from Hell... via Torquay

Voted the best British TV series of all time by the BFI's
industry poll in 2000, *Fawlty Towers'* stock may have slipped
just a touch since then but it still retains "legendary" status.
The show's comic reputation stands on just two six-episode
runs, four years apart. Set in the fictional titular hotel, it
allows the viewer to cackle at the farcical antics and hyper-
tension of epically rude owner Basil Fawlty (heyday Cleese).
He's dominated by his wife Sybil (Scales), and takes out his
Little Englander frustrations on put-upon maid Polly (Booth)
and bumbling Spanish waiter Manuel (Sachs), as well as the
unfortunate guests. Cleese's snobbishness and faux pas only
push him to further depths of desperation.

The show's inspiration came from a Torquay hotel
owner Cleese had witnessed while the Python team were
staying there. So intrigued were he and then-wife Booth
(who co-wrote the first script) that they stayed on to further
observe him. The couple divorced between the two series.
When Richard Ingrams gave the show a bad review in *The
Spectator*, Cleese exacted revenge in the second series by
giving the critic's name to the character caught with a blow-
up doll in his room. The show was a global smash, even in
Spain – once Manuel's nationality was changed to Italian.

Frequent targets included Edward Heath and Richard
Nixon, but the influential Python, moving on to films
and stage shows, has easily outlived both. Aptly, British
citizenship exams now include questions regarding Python
sketches.

If you liked this you'll like:
The Office, Porridge, Monty Python.

THE SWEENEY

CREATED BY:	Ian Kennedy Martin
STARRING:	John Thaw, Dennis Waterman, Garfield Morgan
DATES:	January 1975 – December 1978
SEASONS:	4
EPISODES:	53

SOUNDBITE:

"Look, slag, I don't give a toss who you have in your bed, but don't you try and run your numbers on me!"

DI Jack Regan

REVIEW:

"In the 1970s, this was the only cop show that mattered."

The Guardian

"Get your trousers on – you're nicked"

While now it might appear like a lot of shouting, fighting and boorish macho behaviour, this British police series revolutionised the genre in the 1970s. Jack Regan (Thaw, not yet the more restrained Inspector Morse) is with the Flying Squad (cockney rhyming slang: Sweeney Todd), a branch of the Met specialising in tackling armed robbery and violent crime. Regan and partner DS George Carter (Waterman) are often more underhand and thuggish than the villains, but they got the job done. Usually. In the real world, The Flying Squad was being censured for corruption and bribery: the commander was jailed in 1977. Regan and Carter, in their kipper ties and stained suits, may have been too busy speeding around in Ford Consuls, brawling and boozing, to notice.

However, much as it now looks and sounds like an easy-to-spoof relic, *The Sweeney* – influenced by the 1971 Michael Caine movie *Get Carter!* – broke new ground, scraping away the whitewash and portraying its coppers as real, fallible, men, getting their hands dirty and distinctly unlikely to offer any passers by a cosy "Evening, all." They'd cut corners and cheat the system. The show's action and humour also pushed boundaries, as long as those boundaries were within West London (budget constraints). Two spin-off films tarnished the legacy, but Regan's sneer stayed staunch to the end.

If you liked this you'll like:
The Professionals, Minder, Life On Mars..

SOAP

CREATED BY:	Susan Harris
STARRING:	Katherine Helmond, Richard Mulligan, Billy Crystal, Robert Guillaume
DATES:	September 1977 – April 1981
SEASONS:	4
EPISODES:	85 (93 in syndication)

SOUNDBITE:

"Confused? You won't be after this episode of *Soap!*"

Announcer, (after re-capping the absurdly convoluted plot line at the beginning of every show).

REVIEW:

"A prolonged dirty joke without cleverness or style or subtlety. Its sex jokes are delivered by the shovelful, like manure."

The Los Angeles Times

Good clean fun. Almost

A daring-but-daft, ahead-of-its-time parody of daytime soap operas, *Soap* brought in ludicrous plots involving murder, kidnapping, alien abduction, demonic possession, infidelity, homosexuality, impotence, incest and new age cults – with a knowing nod-and-a-wink to the viewer. It was the first network show ever to have a "viewer discretion" notice for adult themes. Conservatives disliked the "salacious" references to sex and perversion, while gay rights activists argued that the character of Jodie (the then-young comedian Crystal) reinforced negative stereotypes (e.g. his wish to have a sex change). The controversy helped the show become a hit, though when it abruptly ended after four seasons, with cliffhangers unresolved, pressure from advertising agencies and sponsors were to blame. Hindsight has seen praise heaped upon the show's cast (some of whom previously starred on conventional daytime soaps) and writing, with creator Susan Harris going on to produce spin-off *Benson* and *The Golden Girls*.

Notionally "the story of two sisters – Jessica Tate and Mary Campbell", *Soap* features a rich family, a working-class family, mobsters in disguises, handy pleas of temporary insanity, convenient bouts of amnesia, Moonies, prostitutes and oversexed aliens. It was, and remains, like nothing else you've ever seen. After *Soap*, TV had to dirty its hands and raise its game.

If you liked this you'll like:
Benson, The Golden Girls, Murphy Brown.

BOYS FROM THE BLACKSTUFF

CREATED BY:	Alan Bleasdale
STARRING:	Bernard Hill, Michael Angelis, Alan Igbon, Peter Kerrigan
DATES:	January 1980 (play); October – November 1982 (series)
SEASONS:	1
EPISODES:	7 (including original *Play For Today*)

SOUNDBITE:

"Gizza job! I can do that!"

Yosser Hughes

REVIEW:

"A seminal drama series… a warm, humorous but ultimately tragic look at the way economics affect ordinary people."

British Film Institute

Black comedy which raged against the machine

Bleasdale wrote one-off play *The Black Stuff* for the BBC in 1978, but it wasn't screened until 1980. The enthusiastic response it then gained led to the commissioning of the sequel serial, of which Bleasdale had already written a majority. So successful was this that only two months after its initial BBC2 transmission it was shown on BBC1, winning a Bafta award. In a 2000 poll, the BFI placed *Boys from the Blackstuff* in the top ten shows of the twentieth century, eulogising it as, "TV's most dramatic response to the Thatcher era, and a lament to the end of a male working-class British culture".

The introductory play concerns a group of Scouse tarmac-layers (hence: the "blackstuff") on a job in the Middlesbrough area. The subsequent series, filmed mostly in Toxteth, Liverpool, follows the five now-unemployed men. Each episode focuses on the life of a different character (Snowy, Dixie, Chrissie, Yosser, George) as they desperately search for employment, their domestic lives and mental well-being suffering. We witness scams, subterfuge and the persistent battle between the workers and the "sniffers" (benefit fraud investigators). Bonhomie and brisk dialogue abounds, but the last two episodes, in particular, hit operatic heights. Yosser Hughes (Hill, in an iconic role) loses everything and walks the streets on the edge of insanity: flashes of bleak surreal comedy barely dilute the sense of despair. As resonant as ever.

If you liked this you'll like:
Edge Of Darkness, G.B.H., This Is England.

BRIDESHEAD REVISITED

CREATED BY:	Charles Sturridge, Michael Lindsay–Hogg
STARRING:	Jeremy Irons, Anthony Andrews, Diana Quick, Phoebe Nicholls , Laurence Olivier
DATES:	October 1981 – December 1981
SEASONS:	1
EPISODES:	11

SOUNDBITE:

"It seems to me that without your religion Sebastian might have had a chance to be a happy and healthy man."

Charles Ryder

REVIEW:

"The smooth, subdued, masterfully acted series brims with universal themes: love, duty, faith, change, and the mixed pains and pride of family relationships."

The Onion A.V. Club

The big daddy to Downton Abbey

This multi-Bafta-winning ITV adaptation of Evelyn Waugh's 1945 novel now enjoys a reputation carved in stone as one of the all-time British greats. In 2012, this story of "religion, nobility and paisley dressing gowns" was pipped to the post by *The Sopranos* by the narrowest of margins, when *The Guardian* named it the second best TV drama ever.

Yet this shining light of suave elegance had to survive a troubled birth. The first director (Lindsay-Hogg) had to leave halfway through. There were technician strikes and various production delays. Jeremy Irons only agreed to stay on board to finish the job if they'd wait while he went off to shoot *The French Lieutenant's Woman*. The upside of this was that Laurence Olivier now became available to play Lord Marchmain. Before it aired, *Brideshead Revisited* was being whispered about as an expensive, doomed disaster. All the hardship was happily forgotten as the friendship of two young men who first meet at Oxford University in 1922 is told in quiet flashback. Brideshead, Sebastian's (Andrews) family home, is where Charles (Irons) encounters the privileged class and ascends from boy to man in a picturesque, but at times disconcerting, whirl of love, angst and scenic interludes, taking in Morocco and Venice. Waugh's subtle humour and interest in between-the-wars social mores became, surprisingly, catnip to an American audience. In TV terms, *Brideshead Revisited* is *Downton Abbey*'s big daddy.

If you liked this you'll like:
The Forsyte Saga, A Dance To The Music Of Time, The Line Of Beauty.

HILL STREET BLUES

CREATED BY:	Steven Bochco, Michael Kozoll
STARRING:	Daniel J. Travanti, Veronica Hamel, Michael Conrad, Bruce Weitz
DATES:	January 1981 – May 1987
SEASONS:	7
EPISODES:	146

SOUNDBITE:

"Let's do it to them before they do it to us."

Sgt. Stan Jablonski

REVIEW:

"Among the most influential TV shows ever made… its DNA can be found in nearly every great drama produced in the thirty-plus years since it debuted."

Alan Sepinwall

The cop show which re-wrote the rulebook

There's a strong argument that this is where all the good stuff began. If you saw *Hill Street Blues* for the first time now, you might think it played like a set of HBO clichés – but it patented those clichés. As is often with revolutionary shows, rave reviews give way to feeble ratings: "too violent, too sexy, too grim" declared NBC. The show was the original ensemble piece that allowed the audience an insight into an overworked, over-stressed police precinct and follows all the characters – from the captain to the beat cops – and their professional and personal relationships. Using handheld cameras, story arcs that overlapped several episodes, and – as if this wasn't all ground-breaking enough – gave African-American actors key regular roles. *Hill Street Blues* acknowledged the existence of police corruption, racism and alcoholism. In short, it was both the Hendrix and the punk rock of television, making all our contemporary dark, intelligent favourites possible.

This wasn't unrecognised. The show shares the Primetime Emmy-winning record (for Drama Series) with *The West Wing*, *Mad Men* and *L.A. Law*. Mike Post's theme tune also became a hit. Bochco went on to co-create *L.A. Law* and this show's spiritual heir, *NYPD Blue*, among others (like the underrated *Murder One*) and his long-awaited comeback – *Murder In The First* – premieres in 2014.

If you liked this you'll like:
NYPD Blue, *The Shield*, *Murder One*.

CHEERS

CREATED BY:	James Burrows, Glen Charles, Les Charles
STARRING:	Ted Danson, Shelley Long, Kirstie Alley, George Wendt, Woody Harrelson, Kelsey Grammer, Rhea Perlman, John Ratzenberger
DATES:	September 1982 – May 1993
SEASONS:	11
EPISODES:	270

SOUNDBITE:

"To me, our relationship makes perfect sense. You want me to propose to you, I propose to you. You say no, I say fine, I never wanna see you again. You drive me nuts telling me you want me to propose again. I do, you turn me down. It's the classic American love story."

Sam, to Diane

REVIEW:

"What makes the show highly watchable three decades on is the cracking quality of the dialogue, the comic acting and the weird yet likeable characters."

The Telegraph

The comedy where everybody knows your name...

Cheers was a flop, initially. Its first season ratings were in the gutter (74th out of 77 that year), and only good reviews – and the fact that NBC had nothing to replace it with – kept it on air. Eleven seasons and a record number of Emmy nominations later, *Cheers* stands as one of the best-written and most-loved sit-coms ever made, an exemplar for wit, pacing and characterisation.

The regulars at Boston bar Cheers, where everybody knows your name, share their experiences, problems and romances while affectionately mocking each other's flaws and trading acidic repartee. First, ex-pitcher Sam "Mayday" Malone (Danson) has a dysfunctional relationship with Diane (Long), then, when she departs, with Rebecca (Alley). As these symbolic gender wars rage, lampooning sexual stereotypes, we come to genuinely care about all three.

Cheers miraculously survived the exit of key players: nobody thought it could out-live Sam and Diane, but Sam and Rebecca's relationship gave the show a whole new world of tragi-comedy. When Woody (Harrelson) joined the bar staff, ratings rocketed. Idle barfly Norm's beer-nuts and Cliff's informative trivia, Carla's sharp tongue, the fretting Frasier (the nonpareil of spin-offs) and icy Lilith: these characters remain the gold standard against which all ensembles shall be judged. Its farewell was the most watched show that year. Taking a break from all your troubles sure can help a lot.

If you liked this you'll like:
Frasier, Barney Miller, Friends.

BLACKADDER

WRITTEN BY:	Richard Curtis, Rowan Atkinson (series 1), Ben Elton (series 2–4)
STARRING:	Rowan Atkinson, Tony Robinson, Tim McInnerny, Miranda Richardson, Hugh Laurie, Stephen Fry
DATES:	June 1983 – November 1989
SEASONS:	4
EPISODES:	24 (plus 3 specials)

SOUNDBITE:

"Am I jumping the gun, Baldrick, or are the words 'I have a cunning plan' marching with ill-deserved confidence in the direction of this conversation?"

Edmund Blackadder

REVIEW:

"Curtis admits things didn't settle down until Elton came on board as co-writer for series two, the Elizabethan one. The show retreated into cardboard sets, but developed an ease and swagger it would never lose."

The Guardian

"I think the phrase rhymes with clucking bell!"

Blackadder is the umbrella name for the four series of the renowned "period sitcom", which drop-kicked its two protagonists – Atkinson's antihero Edmund Blackadder and sidekick-dogsbody Baldrick (Robinson) – into different historical conflicts. The first, *The Black Adder*, lands in an alternative late Middle Ages; *Blackadder II* ridicules the Elizabethan era. *Blackadder The Third* romps with the Regency period, while the darker *Blackadder Goes Forth* finds our cunning pair cowering on the Western Front during WWI. It is a rare poll of British sitcom fans which doesn't find *Blackadder* competing with *Only Fools And Horses* for top spot; though the show usually wins "best put-down", with phrases such as "the eyes are open, the mouth moves, but Mr Brain has long since departed, hasn't he, Percy?" Atkinson, Curtis, Fry, Laurie and Elton all went on to bigger – though not indisputably better – things. Conceived during *Not The Nine O'clock News* writing sessions, *Blackadder*'s first series, with its mockery of the Crusades, witchcraft and Shakespearean dialogue enjoyed a relatively high budget. As *Blackadder* progressed the ages, it became clear its strengths were wit and irreverence, rather than costumes and expensive locations. And let us not forget the late Rik Mayall's unhinged, bravura appearances as Lord Flashheart, a highlight of every series. The show's affecting finale – "Goodbyeee" – went boldly over the top.

If you liked this you'll like:
Jeeves & Wooster, Mr. Bean, House M.D.

SEINFELD

CREATED BY:	Jerry Seinfeld, Larry David
STARRING:	Jerry Seinfeld, Jason Alexander, Julia Louis-Dreyfus, Michael Richards
DATES:	July 1989 – May 1998
SEASONS:	9
EPISODES:	180

KEY QUOTE:

"It became very clear to me sitting out there today that every decision I've made in my entire life has been wrong. My life is the complete opposite of everything I want it to be."

George Costanza

REVIEW:

"Seinfeld's gentle humour is easy to take. Unlike other current comedians, such as Andrew Dice Clay or Sam Kinison, Seinfeld isn't angry: he's more awed by the wonder of it all."

Newsday

Nineties narcissism breeds comedy classic

Commonly described as "a show about nothing", with "no hugging or learning", *Seinfeld* ruled the Nineties: a commercial giant as well as post-modern critics' favourite. It shared the top two positions on the ratings with *ER* every year from '94 to '98. Jerry Seinfeld has suggested it was a show about how comedians get their material, and famously conceived it with best friend Larry David, who went on to further acclaim with *Curb Your Enthusiasm*. The show was set around Seinfeld's New York apartment and nearby diner, where a neurotic "version" of himself experienced comic misadventures with his equally narcissistic friend George (Alexander, playing a caricature of David) and ex-girlfriend Elaine (Louis-Dreyfus).

The show offered Jerry as the reasonable centre among this insecure, rootless, self-obsessed group – despite his peculiar reasons for finding fault with a steady flow of girlfriends, from an irritating laugh to large hands to eating peas one at a time. Elaine was pompous and over-candid; George petty and envious. Deathless episodes include "The Contest", "The Soup Nazi", "The Boyfriend" and "The Parking Garage". *Seinfeld*, named as the greatest show of all time by *TV Guide* in 2013, displayed a reassuring and refreshing lack of faith in humanity, and, as many pop-psychologists declared, remains a watershed moment in the self-referential muddying of lines between reality and fiction, yada yada yada…

If you liked this you'll like:
Curb Your Enthusiasm, Veep, Louie.

THE SIMPSONS

CREATED BY:	Matt Groening
STARRING:	(Voices) Dan Castellaneta, Julie Kavner, Nancy Cartwright, Yeardley Smith, Hank Azaria
DATES:	December 1989 – present
SEASONS:	25
EPISODES:	552

SOUNDBITE:

Lisa: "Dad, just for once don't you want to try something new?"
Homer: "Oh Lisa, trying is just the first step toward failure."

REVIEW:

"The American family at its most complicated, drawn as simple cartoons. It's this neat paradox that makes millions concentrate on *The Simpsons* …a pop-cultural phenomenon."

Entertainment Weekly

We are all yellow...the family, devalued

An animated sitcom following the satirical adventures of a dysfunctional working-class family in Springfield. That doesn't quite cover it. *The Simpsons* has become, from humble origins, so much more over a quarter-century at the top: cultural touchstone, arch commentator, punk prophet, the anti-Waltons. Its garish yellow ray-gun has levelled society, hypocrisy…and television itself.

It gives us, of course, Homer, the patron saint of lazy buffoons and lousy beer-swilling fathers; Marge, his more diligent wife; their boy Bart, proud under-achiever, and his younger sister Lisa, the undervalued intellectual prodigy. Oh, and Maggie, the silent baby. Groening named the clan after his own (substituting Bart for Matt). Short skits for *The Tracy Ullman Show* became a half-hour show and then Fox's first major hit. It's now the longest-running US sitcom *and* the longest-running US scripted primetime series, spawning a movie, a star on the Hollywood Walk of Fame and numerous catchphrases, not least Homer's expressive "D'oh!"

It may seem effortless, but each episode takes six months to produce. Spanning over 500 episodes (and counting) the show has tackled, with genuine wit and emotion, important real life dilemmas such as green issues, nuclear power, adultery, politics, corruption, education, global finance, evil corporations, religion and, of course, those "cheese-eating surrender monkeys".

If you liked this you'll like:
Futurama, Family Guy, King Of The Hill.

TWIN PEAKS

CREATED BY:	David Lynch, Mark Frost
STARRING:	Kyle MacLachlan, Sheryl Lee, Sherilyn Fenn, Ray Wise
DATES:	April 1990 – June 1991
SEASONS:	2
EPISODES:	30

SOUNDBITE:

"I have no idea where this will lead us, but I have a definite feeling it will be a place both wonderful and strange."

Dale Cooper

REVIEW:

"*Twin Peaks* disorients you in ways that small-screen productions seldom attempt. It's a pleasurable sensation."

Washington Post

David Lynch's surreal masterpiece

For all its non-linear nebulousness and surrealism, *Twin Peaks* was one of the biggest shows of 1990, cheered on by critics who totally "got it" (or, if they didn't, were damn well going to pretend to). Its cult fan base won it a second series – a development that Lynch and Frost probably hadn't anticipated: the drop in writing quality and confidence certainly suggests they were winging it later on. Declining viewer figures led the network, ABC, to insist that Laura Palmer's (Lee) murderer be revealed halfway through the season.

As with most of Lynch's work, *Twin Peaks* defies genre placement and floats unsettlingly between campy horror and unhinged soap opera. Like the acclaimed *Blue Velvet*, it lifts a rock and offers a close-up on what crawls out, probing the seedy underbelly of small-town respectability. If a character doesn't lead a bizarre double life, they're in the wrong show.

The puzzling death of homecoming queen Laura in the pilot provides the mystery which Agent Dale Cooper (MacLachlan) is required to solve, and sparks a chain reaction of odd events. Drugs, sex, dreams, Killer Bob, the Log Lady and The Man From Another Place play their part. Both seasons end on edge-of-seat cliffhangers. "Lynchean" may be the most gratuitously overused adjective in the history of film criticism, but if you seek the very essence of Lynch, it resides in *Twin Peaks*.

If you liked this you'll like:
Rubicon, The X-Files, Lost.

PRIME SUSPECT

CREATED BY:	Lynda La Plante
STARRING:	Helen Mirren, Tom Bell, John Benfield, Mark Strong
DATES:	April 1991 – October 2006
SEASONS:	7
EPISODES:	15

SOUNDBITE:

"Listen, I like to be called Governor or Boss. I don't like Ma'am – I'm not the bloody Queen. So take your pick."

DCI Jane Tennison

REVIEW:

"The acting in *Prime Suspect* has a natural feel, aided by moments of improvisation, and the mystery is grounded in reality, not the fantastical."

The Onion A.V. Club

Mirren takes no prisoners

What the over-tired word "gritty" was invented for. When in 1991 Mirren appeared for the first time as DCI Jane Tennison, TV police procedurals were not commonly unglamorous. In the States, *Hill Street Blues* had tested the waters. By the time Mirren departed fifteen years later (there were often long breaks between the seven short but intense series), TV producers was competing to "out-dark" each other, and, to this day, still continue to (see *The Killing*). Lynda La Plante's creation proved influential on both sides of the Atlantic, inspiring a long-list of forensic cop shows from *CSI* and *The Closer to Life On Mars*… to *anything* with a strong female lead.

No-nonsense Tennison has to survive and negotiate in a male-dominated profession, where, sick of being passed over for cases, she lands a sensational murder investigation which proves anything but a slam-dunk, thus nurturing the resentment from sexist colleagues. At this time, there were only four female DCIs in Britain (one helped as advisor to the writers). Later series' shifted the spotlight to specific "issues", from child abuse to racism to prostitution. Tennison isn't painted (by Mirren or La Plante) as a crusading saint: arrogance, an inability to find a work-life balance and (later) alcoholism cramp her talent. As a testament to Mirren's acting, one of the show's editors proudly claimed that their mantra was: "If in doubt, cut to Helen".

If you liked this you'll like:
The Closer, Cracker, The Fall.

THE LARRY SANDERS SHOW

CREATED BY:	Garry Shandling, Dennis Klein
STARRING:	Shandling, Jeffrey Tambor, Rip Torn, Janeane Garofalo
DATES:	August 1992 – May 1998
SEASONS:	6
EPISODES:	89

SOUNDBITE:

"Thank you very much: no flipping."

Larry

REVIEW:

"A comedy series so funny and risqué as to make *Seinfeld* look positively bland."

The New York Times

The greatest TV show... about a TV show

The pioneering, brutally funny fictional talk show has been hailed as "the greatest HBO sitcom of all time", and "the closest a sitcom ever came to perfect pitch". As well as establishing HBO's reputation for quality television, its innovations included taking the camera backstage (inspiring *30 Rock, Studio 60 on the Sunset Strip*), following characters as they walk and talk (inspiring *ER, The West Wing*), and persuading celebrities to portray themselves unflatteringly (you name it). Without Larry Sanders there may have been no Alan Partridge. And without the show's squirms of mortifying awkwardness there may have been no *The Office, Curb Your Enthusiasm* or *Arrested Development*. "This is where it all began", wrote *The Guardian*, "the whole postmodernist, self-reflexive, fact-fiction sitcom thing."

   Larry's late-night chat show was a progression from Shandling's earlier sitcom, *It's Garry Shandling's Show* (1986-90), which continuously broke the fourth wall. Larry is an insecure egomaniac, enabled by producer Artie (Torn) and whipping-boy sidekick Hank "Hey now!" Kingsley (Tambor). Our self-loathing host, under pressure to go more commercial, go younger, go broader, alienates all and teeters on the brink of implosion. During the final episode, Sean Penn, during an ad break, lays into Larry's acting in *Hurlyburly* (a film in which they'd both appeared) as well as his attitude towards Penn's wife. Many shows owe a debt to Sanders, though few have cut as deep. Larry's last words in his show-within-a-show are: "You may now flip."

If you liked this you'll like:
Knowing Me Knowing You, Curb Your Enthusiasm, Extras.

NYPD BLUE

CREATED BY:	Steven Bochco, David Milch
STARRING:	Dennis Franz, David Caruso, Jimmy Smits, Rick Schroder, Kim Delaney
DATES:	September 1993 – March 2005
SEASONS:	12
EPISODES:	261

SOUNDBITE:

"I'm gonna have such a migraine tonight because I didn't beat you."

Andy Sipowicz

REVIEW:

"Take away the nude lovemaking scene, the reactionary potent cussing, the premeditated shock elements… and *NYPD Blue* remains one helluva cop show."

Chicago Sun Times

Often imitated, never bettered

An ensemble cast with up-and-down love lives and
fluctuating job satisfaction in a Manhattan police precinct:
so far, so familiar from *Hill Street Blues* creator Bochco.
But with David Milch's writing based on his friendship
with a real New York cop (who became one of the show's
producers), *NYPD Blue* took everything further, fearlessly.
At first conceived as a vehicle for the glacial David Caruso,
it morphed after his departure into a study of Franz's Andy
Sipowicz, who, across twelve years, evolved from prejudiced,
aggressive drunk to sage mentor. With Franz never playing
for sympathy and unafraid to alienate, he remains one of the
most fully-drawn, complex characters in US TV history. Over
the seasons, calmer, more suave partners came and went
– Smits'Bobby, Schroder's Danny, Mark-Paul Gosselaar's
John – but each time you thought the drama might jump the
shark, it revitalised brilliantly.

In his home life, Sipowicz suffered many tragedies,
and the viewer, tense, waited for him to implode, and the
breakneck saga hummed to a moving finale. *NYPD Blue*
was, absurdly, slammed as everything from "soft porn" to
"profanity", and perfectionist Milch's last-minute dialogue
changes infuriated many cast members. Yet it became ABC's
longest-running primetime drama series, bringing in some
fast-thinking female cops, and bestrode the years either side
of the millennium like a colossus.

If you liked this you'll like:
Homicide: Life On The Street, Hill Street Blues, The Wire.

CRACKER

CREATED BY:	Jimmy McGovern
STARRING:	Robbie Coltrane, Geraldine Somerville, Christopher Eccleston, Ricky Tomlinson
DATES:	September 1993 – November 1995 (Specials 1996 & 2006)
SEASONS:	3
EPISODES:	25

SOUNDBITE:

"I drink too much, I smoke too much, I gamble too much. I *am* too much."

Fitz

REVIEW:

"[Cracker's] a man who can pick his way into the most psychotic of psyches, but forever shirks a wrestle with his own plentiful demons."

Total Film

McGovern, Abbott and Coltrane go deep

Jimmy McGovern and Paul Abbott are two of the most significant British writers/producers of the last two decades. McGovern has given us challenging works like *The Lakes*, *The Street* and *The Accused*, while Abbott has created *Shameless*, *Clocking Off* and *State of Play*. Both contributed to the complexity and grit of *Cracker*, with McGovern writing most of the early episodes plus the controversial "Men Should Weep", and Abbott producing the second series and penning most of the others.

Coltrane's Dr Eddie "Fitz" Fitzgerald is an abrasively eccentric forensic psychologist who helps to solve tough police cases, though often by getting inside the heads of his subjects he opens up as many of his own wounds and insecurities as he does of theirs. The Scottish actor was better known for broad comedy before being cast against type in this intense study of psychosis. A classic anti-hero (perhaps a subsequent influence on the comparatively more cuddly House M.D.), he doesn't shirk from swearing, sarcasm and wanton provocation. Cases often begin with the viewer knowing whodunnit, but draw their tension from whether Fitz and colleagues will tidy things up or make them worse. Fitz's relationships with his wife and with DS Jane Penhaligon (Somerville) are also dysfunctional. McGovern's three-parter "To Be A Somebody", touching on *The Sun*'s coverage of the Hillsborough disaster and serving as Robert Carlyle's breakthrough role, is a seminal 90s work.

If you liked this you'll like:
The Lakes, The Street, State of Play.

THE X-FILES

CREATED BY:	Chris Carter
STARRING:	David Duchovny, Gillian Anderson, Robert Patrick, Mitch Pileggi
DATES:	September 1993 – May 2002
SEASONS:	9
EPISODES:	202

SOUNDBITE:

"I've often felt that dreams are answers to questions we haven't yet figured out how to ask."

Agent Fox Mulder

REVIEW:

"A paean to oddballs, sci-fi fans, conspiracy theorists and Area 51 pilgrims everywhere."

Entertainment Weekly

Occult hit. The truth is out there

Possibly the cult show of cult shows, *The X-Files* was a pop-culture giant of the Nineties. The believer-versus-sceptic odd-couple dynamic of Fox Mulder (Duchovny) and Scully (Anderson), with its subtle undercurrent of sexual tension, has been hugely influential. Despite losing momentum a little in later seasons, the show was ahead of the curve in common use of mobile phones, e-mails and the internet, and one of the first to benefit from website popularity, where fans called themselves X-Philes.

Relatively restrained in terms of sci-fi/horror hybrids, it saw two FBI special agents investigating "x-files" – unsolved, marginalised cases involving paranormal phenomena. Gently eccentric Mulder believes in aliens; cool, rational Scully prefers to make scientific analyses. They are quickly thrust into trusting only each other, their platonic relationship dancing on the brink of something more. There are "monster of the week"-type stand-alone episodes, but all along and throughout the mythology simmers. Tapping into topical suspicions about leaders and governments, *The X-Files* outgrew its left-field "twilight zone" box and ballooned into a runaway monster hit, making Hollywood stars of its principals. The show spawned two feature-length films, and is the longest-running American sci-fi series ever (albeit was filmed in Vancouver for the first five seasons). Strong in both plot and character development, *The X-Files* was as twitchily paranoid as it was slyly subversive.

If you liked this you'll like:
The 4400, Lost, Roswell.

FRASIER

CREATED BY:	David Angell, Peter Casey, David Lee
STARRING:	Kelsey Grammer, David Hyde Pierce, Jane Leeves, John Mahoney
DATES:	September 1993 – May 2004
SEASONS:	11
EPISODES:	264

SOUNDBITE:

"And though washing one's hands twenty to thirty times a day might be considered obsessive-compulsive, please bear in mind that your husband is a coroner. Thank you for your call. Roz, whom do we have next?"

Frasier

REVIEW:

"Inspired by the classic comedies of manners, as were the frequent deflations of Frasier's pomposity."

NBC News

The sardonic spin-off which bucked the trend

Frasier is responding helpfully to a caller: "Roger, at Cornell University they have this incredible piece of scientific equipment known as the Tunnelling Electron Microscope. Now, this microscope is so powerful that by firing electrons you can actually see images of the atom, the infinitesimally minute building blocks of our universe. Roger, if I were using that microscope right now, I still wouldn't be able to locate my interest in your problem."

Eminent psychiatrist Dr Frasier Crane has left the Cheers bar behind, and now has a radio show in Seattle, where he dispenses insight and wisdom to his listeners. Free of Lilith (his dragon-ex), he's set on a new bachelor life, but there are hindrances. At home, he is a wordy wreck, compelled to share an apartment with his retired-cop father Martin (Mahoney) and his dad's carer Daphne (the curiously-accented Leeves). Frasier's fey, aesthetically-inclined brother Niles often pops over, creating an onscreen relationship akin to a thinking man's Laurel and Hardy. Even more hilarious, when you consider Frasier once told his friends at Cheers that he was an only child.

One of the most successful spin-off shows in history, *Frasier* made Grammer the highest-paid TV actor in the States, and Leeves the highest-paid British actress. Lightning wit, chemistry and perfect timing helped Frasier break *The Mary Tyler Moore Show's* record for Primetime Emmys.

If you liked this you'll like:
Cheers, Will And Grace, Friends.

FRIENDS

CREATED BY:	David Crane, Marta Kauffman
STARRING:	Jennifer Aniston, Courteney Cox, Lisa Kudrow, Matthew Perry, David Schwimmer, Matt LeBlanc
DATES:	September 1994 – May 2004
SEASONS:	10
EPISODES:	236

SOUNDBITE:

"First divorce: wife's hidden sexuality, not my fault. Second divorce: said the wrong name at the altar, kind of my fault. Third divorce: they shouldn't let you get married when you're that drunk and have stuff drawn all over your face, Nevada's fault."

Ross

REVIEW:

"*Friends* hands us one more batch of quirky, single, more-or-less charming twenty-somethings and lets them hang for a half-hour reading faux Woody Allen lines."

San Diego Union-Tribune

They'll be there for you

"The lives, loves and laughs of six young friends living in Manhattan" – it sounds like a cheese-ball sitcom cliché now, but *Friends* was the Rolls-Royce of the genre. Despite frequent lapses into cutesiness and sentimentality, it's generally much funnier than you remember: as the constant worldwide syndication demonstrates. Although tastes have taken a darker, more misanthropic turn since the new millennium, those six friends and their intertwining relationships remain as buoyant a feature of the comedy textbook as the mockumentary format or Basil Fawlty's tantrums.

Friends has entered the cultural lexicon. Jennifer Aniston's "Rachel" haircut, Joey's "How you doin'?" catchphrase, Chandler's sarcasm, the use of an extended "so" as an emphatic adjective… all these have been adopted as societal norms, their impact and popularity analysed by academics. The gang also represented the new family, as modern urban dwellers ditched tradition and instead choose their nearest and dearest confidantes rather than stick passively with relatives. Rachel's dating debacles, Monica's competitive perfectionism, Phoebe's ditziness and bad songs ("Smelly Cat"), Joey's womanising and hammy acting, Chandler's weird upbringing and Ross's sweet awkwardness have been hugely influential far beyond the boundaries of Central Perk café. The show's farewell was the fourth most watched finale ever, behind only *M*A*S*H*, *Cheers* and *Seinfeld*.

If you liked this you'll like:
New Girl, Coupling, The Big Bang Theory.

THE DAY TODAY

CREATED BY:	Chris Morris, Armando Iannucci
STARRING:	Chris Morris, Steve Coogan, Rebecca Front, Doon Mackichan
DATES:	January 1994 – February 1994
SEASONS:	1
EPISODES:	6

SOUNDBITE:

"The Day Today – slamming the wasps from the pure apple of truth."

Announcer

REVIEW:

"This beats them all. It's the degree of detail that makes it special: not a single frame goes by that is not biting at some aspect of television news."

BBC News

All the news that matters...

Its unsettling successor *Brass Eye* is favoured by many, but *The Day Today* is the stew of satire and surrealism that launched the TV careers of resoundingly influential *enfants terribles* Chris Morris, Steve Coogan and Armando Iannucci, as well as introducing Patrick Marber, Rebecca Front and many other key players in the hard-hitting "post-alternative" comedy landmark of the mid-90s. Ostensibly a spoof of network news, it digs deep at the conventional presentation of same: the media's manner of depicting social crises amid inappropriate everyday sensationalism. Ludicrous, blatantly fictitious stories are covered with a mock-earnest "professional" attitude, loose-anchored by Morris. There are swerves into phoney trailers and soap operas, and the prescient banality and futility of the vox-pop, "Speak Your Brains".

Morris' RokTV segment spoofs MTV, giving us the psychotic rapper Fur Q, while Mackichan's business correspondent Collaterlie Sisters spews meaningless jargon over bewildering graphics and Marber's Patrick O'Hanraha-hanrahan is an incompetent, petulant economics "expert". Morris zealously insults his colleagues, including a young-ish sports reporter, Alan Partridge ("Join me").

Adapted from radio show *On The Hour*, *The Day Today* lampooned media hypocrisy and hysteria while managing a few good sketches too. It seems more uncannily accurate today than ever.

If you liked this you'll like:
Brass Eye, The Fast Show, Nathan Barley.

ER

CREATED BY:	Michael Crichton
STARRING:	Anthony Edwards, George Clooney, Julianna Margulies, Noah Wyle, Eriq LaSalle
DATES:	September 1994 – April 2009
SEASONS:	15
EPISODES:	331

SOUNDBITE:

"I've been doing this job for seventeen years, honey. Doctors come and go, but nurses make this place run. We see a lot of misery and dying, but we come back every day."

Nurse Adams

REVIEW:

"A trauma-rama that opens on an adrenaline rush and pretty much stays there, with time-outs for pathos, sex and dark hilarity."

USA Today

The matron of all hospital dramas

In 1994, Crichton, an ex-physician, became the only man ever to have his works simultaneously go to number one in the US film, book and TV charts. (*Jurassic Park*, *Disclosure* and *ER*, since you asked).

ER is the most Emmy-nominated drama in history, with a staggering total of 124 nominations. Fifteen seasons, at that level, is another mindboggling statistic, unlikely ever to be beaten. And its success wasn't solely down to George Clooney, appearing in his breakthrough acting role as the original Dr McDreamy, Doug Ross.

Following the frenetic whirl of an ER (Emergency Room) in a fictional Chicago hospital, the stories balance medical cases faced by the ER team with their personal lives. Although the studio head was worried that *St. Elsewhere* had mined similar seams, with Steven Spielberg as a producer *ER* took off like a rocket, seeing off David E. Kelley's rival *Chicago Hope*. While the show might compress time (a 24-hour shift might last one 48-minute episode), real-life doctors agreed that, generally, it remained surprisingly accurate to medical reality.

Then of course there were the love stories. Clooney and Margulies weren't the only subsequent big name stars to pull a double shift. In various seasons, Maria Bello, Goran Višnji and Angela Bassett donned the scrubs too. Social issues were addressed. Deaths of major characters drew huge, sobbing, audiences worldwide. Lists of the best TV shows ever which elect not to include *ER* are exceedingly rare.

If you liked this you'll like:
Grey's Anatomy, St. Elsewhere, Chicago Hope.

OUR FRIENDS IN THE NORTH

CREATED BY:	Peter Flannery
STARRING:	Christopher Eccleston, Daniel Craig, Gina McKee, Mark Strong
DATES:	January 1996 – March 1996
SEASONS:	1
EPISODES:	9

SOUNDBITE:

"Our story began one summer night in 1964, as I came back to see me friends. I can see now, 31 years later, we were all going to make decisions that would change our lives forever."

Nicky Hutchinson (narrating)

REVIEW:

"Captivated much of the country, sketching a panoramic view of life in Britain from the 60s to the 90s. At once sweeping and intimate, moving and angry, historical and contemporary."

The Independent

Stars are born amid the fog on the Tyne...

Named by *The Guardian* as the third greatest British TV drama of all time, *Our Friends*...was first written by Flannery as a three-hour play, which ran up to 1979 and Margaret Thatcher's coming to power. BBC producer Michael Wearing, who'd worked on 1982's classic *Boys from the Blackstuff*, saw the show's potential as an epic regional drama. Worries about litigation concerning the real-life scandals involved were overcome after much delay. Ultimately, Flannery felt the hold-ups benefited the project, as he extended the story into the Nineties, bringing the four central characters into middle age.

The nine-part series followed the fortunes of four friends. Each episode was set in a different year, as the quartet's personal lives became entangled with the political struggles of Newcastle (their home town) and London. Around them the viewer witnesses the effects of bureaucratic sleaze, police corruption, slum housing deals, the rise of Thatcherism and the 1984-85 Miners' Strike. The writer's vision prevailed, and the controversial, compelling and profoundly poignant series offered "lives imagined in emotional detail" (*The Independent*). "We are not likely to look upon its like again", suggested *The Telegraph*.

The show also introduced four now households celebrities: future James Bond, Daniel Craig, future Doctor Who, Christopher Eccleston, and the equally impressive Mark Strong and Gina McKee.

If you liked this you'll like:
Boys from the Blackstuff, Holding On, White Heat, Heimat.

SOUTH PARK

CREATED BY:	Trey Parker, Matt Stone
STARRING:	(Voices): Trey Parker, Matt Stone, Isaac Hayes, Mona Marshall
DATES:	August 1997 – present
SEASONS:	17 (Season 18 to air in 2014)
EPISODES:	247

SOUNDBITE:

"Wow, cartoons are getting really dirty."

Stan

REVIEW:

"Undeniably fearless lampooning of all that is self-important and hypocritical in American life."

The Peabody Awards

The irreverent town where everthing goes South...

"The following programme contains coarse language and due to its content it should not be viewed by anyone."

And so it begins, the "shock-humour" black comedy satire which started life as two crudely animated shorts that went viral on the relatively young internet. *South Park* is now acknowledged as the show that put Comedy Central on the map, and led to the channel growing from an infiltration of nine million households in 1997 to 50 million a year later. *South Park* has spawned countless catchphrases, a feature-length film-musical and, of course, much controversy for its scattergun cussing and take-no-prisoners war against both political correctness and its opponents. What's it rebelling against? Whaddya got?

We first meet irreverent schoolboys Stan, Kyle, Eric and Kenny as they undergo bizarre misadventures in the titular Colorado town, USA. From there, all safety guards are off, as some episode names might suggest: "Cartman Gets An Anal Probe", "Cartman's Mom Is A Dirty Slut", "With Apologies to Jesse Jackson". Toilet humour is used to offend all sensibilities, especially the religious. Even late cast member Isaac Hayes (a Scientologist, and voice of Chef) found Parker and Stone's debunking of Scientology as "a big fat global scam" too much, and promptly hung up his chocolate salty balls. The Buddha-snorting-cocaine episode prompted a blanket ban of the show in Sri Lanka. Parker and Stone claim to hate conservatives and liberals equally.

If you liked this you'll like:
Futurama, Robot Chicken, The Oblongs.

I'M ALAN PARTRIDGE

CREATED BY:	Steve Coogan, Armando Iannucci, Peter Baynham
STARRING:	Steve Coogan, Felicity Montagu, Simon Greenall, Sally Phillips
DATES:	November 1997 – December 2002
SEASONS:	2
EPISODES:	12

SOUNDBITE:

"I know lying is wrong, but if the elephant man came in now, in a blouse, with some make-up on and said, 'How do I look?' would you say... 'Go and take that blusher off, you mis-shapen-headed elephant tranny'? No. You'd say, 'You look nice … John.'"

Alan Partridge

REVIEW:

"Alan's back and life is on the up. He's got the third best slot on Radio Norwich, a girlfriend and a Lexus. Back of the net!"

tv.com

Bouncing Back... Alan's autobiography is a classic

You'll of course remember Alan Partridge from his TV chat show *Knowing Me Knowing You*, from which he was dropped for all-round out-of-touch incompetence and, most pertinently, for punching the BBC's chief commissioning editor in the face. Now divorced, living in the Linton Travel Tavern, and hosting the graveyard shift on Radio Norwich, Alan remains convinced he can claw his way back to the top. By series two, a few years on, Alan's bounced back from a nervous breakdown, but remains spirited and rich in denial. Now hosting a military-based quiz show on a digital channel, Alan has high hopes for his autobiography. He also has a younger Ukrainian girlfriend, Sonia, with whom he lives in a caravan outside his only-partially-built dream home.

Coogan and co's blundering, but-all-too-believable comic creation – first sighted in *The Day Today* – is now established as one of Britain's funniest TV characters. Alan's insensitivity, casual chauvinism and deluded fantasies lead to many moments of genius, both farcical and finely nuanced. Has there ever been a more instinctive, inspired riff set in a car park than his shouting repeatedly, and vainly, after "Dan"? Coogan has proven his versatility with equally unsparing dissections of the midlife-male psyche through other, less universally-acclaimed characters, but Partridge remains the emperor of the comedy of embarrassment. A-ha!

If you liked this you'll like:
Knowing Me Knowing You With Alan Partridge, Saxondale, Nighty Night.

OZ

CREATED BY:	Tom Fontana
STARRING:	Ernie Hudson, J.K. Simmons, Lee Tergesen, Harold Perrineau Jr
DATES:	July 1997 – February 2003
SEASONS:	6
EPISODES:	56

SOUNDBITE:

"Oz. The name on the street for the Oswald State Correctional Facility, Level 4."

Augustus Hill

REVIEW:

"Unpleasant to watch, gruesome, claustrophobic… yet serious, disturbing and gripping."

The New York Times

We're not in Kansas any more, Toto...

"Oz" is a fictional maximum-security prison in New York State. The tagline for the show ran "It's no place like home". In its experimental unit – Emerald City – rehab and learning during incarceration are emphasised, but fights for power among the racial and social divisions are more standard. Wheelchair-bound narrator Augustus Hill (Harold Perrineau Jr) gives some context, analysis and much-needed humour.

As the first one-hour drama series produced by premium cable network HBO, *Oz* would command a place in history even without its own merits. It made the most of its freedom from traditional TV constraints, with violence, nudity, drug use, swearing and a parade of other taboo-busters.

Oz was often received as tortuously intense or graphic, cheap thrills: The show has its champions and its detractors. There can be no denying it blew the bloody doors off, allowing *The Sopranos*, and others, to rush through and engage a modified audience. Tom Fontana claimed he first thought up the prison drama "almost as a lark", but its harrowing setting was where HBO realized how far it could push things away from feelgood, cosy endings and quaintly moral lessons learned. Fontana wrote and produced the gritty *Homicide: Life on the Street*, before becoming frustrated at NBC's pressure to tweak it into more commercial shapes. *Oz* was defiantly grim, and kick-started new tastes for depth.

If you liked this you'll like:
The Shield, The Sopranos, Orange is the New Black.

BUFFY THE VAMPIRE SLAYER

CREATED BY:	Joss Whedon
STARRING:	Sarah Michelle Gellar, Nicholas Brendon, David Boreanaz, James Marsters, Alyson Hannigan
DATES:	March 1997 – May 2003
SEASONS:	7
EPISODES:	144

SOUNDBITE:

"I'm just worried this whole session's gonna turn into some training montage from an 1980s movie."

Buffy

REVIEW:

"*Buffy* has yet to be taken seriously… yet the show is a knockout: as much as *The West Wing*, it demonstrates what television can accomplish."

The New York Times

Joss Whedon raises the stakes

What if – Joss Whedon, future director of the *Avengers Assemble* franchise, wondered – the girl *isn't* afraid of the monster? What if the monster needs to worry about the strength and powers of the girl? And with that one paradigm shift, the female role in TV dramas was radically altered for a new generation and beyond.

Buffy was a slow-to-grow cult-phenomenon, which overcame the false start of a drippy movie of the same name to become the smartest, sassiest show on TV, loaded with post-modern wit and surprise. Its gang of characters – the Scooby gang – critiqued their own performances and transformations. Buffy (Gellar), Spike, Giles, Willow and Anya were as conflicted, multivalent, sexy, funny and intriguing as any more overtly grown-up HBO leads, while the narrative threads – once Whedon realized how much he could get away with – got darker and deeper, toying mischievously with the concept of Hell. Stand-alone episodes like "Once More, With Feeling" (a musical wholly written by Whedon, and a triumph) or "Hush" (two-thirds of which was silent, because Whedon wished to show he could do more than pen whip-snappy dialogue), took the viewer's breath away in both their ambition and execution.

An extended metaphor for the anxieties of adolescence, a template for a new breed of "knowing" supernatural tales and teen ensembles, and a web of life-and-death love stories: *Buffy* inspired laughs, tears and devotion.

If you liked this you'll like:
Angel, Dollhouse, Tru Calling.

SEX AND THE CITY

CREATED BY:	Darren Star
STARRING:	Sarah Jessica Parker, Kim Cattrall, Kristin Davis, Cynthia Nixon
DATES:	June 1998 – February 2004
SEASONS:	6
EPISODES:	94

SOUNDBITE:

Miranda: "What's the big mystery? It's my clitoris, not the sphinx."
Carrie: "I think you just found the title of your autobiography."

REVIEW:

"*Sex and the City* is to feminism what sugar is to dental care."

The Daily Telegraph

The New Wave of feminism... or its death knell?

Much discussed in the media, *Sex and the City* was both championed as cutting-edge feminism and decried as the death of same. Originating from Candace Bushnell's book (compiled from her *New York Observer* columns), it saw her alter ego Carrie Bradshaw (Parker) and three friends (in their mid-thirties and forties) confiding in each other their combustible sex lives. Gleamingly modern, risqué, and riddled with expensive lifestyle advertising, it embraced frank language and broached such topics as promiscuity, menstruation, safe sex and embarrassing bedroom scenarios.

Carrie, entangled with Mr Big (Chris Noth), narrates (in TV's most unnecessary voiceover), spelling things out in case we're distracted by the footwear. Samantha (Cattrall, the show's real star) is confident and voracious, a self-confessed "try-sexual" (she'll try anything). Charlotte (Davis) is optimistic that true love exists and seeks a knight in shining armour. Miranda (Nixon) is a more cynical voice of reason.

Spawning two commercially successful films (and a short-lived prequel series), *SATC* was a popular culture phenomenon that polarised opinion. Never mind the sex, or even the constant message that what a woman needs is a man: some found the real obscenity lay in its craven materialism. Others simply lapped it up. Recently, *Glamour* magazine remarked upon Carrie's "brattiness", "self-absorption" and "awesome shoes".

If you liked this you'll like:
Friends, Will & Grace, Cougar Town.

FAMILY GUY

CREATED BY:	Seth MacFarlane
STARRING:	(Voices): Seth MacFarlane, Alex Borstein, Mila Kunis, Seth Green
DATES:	January 1999 – November 2003; May 2005 – present
SEASONS:	12
EPISODES:	231

SOUNDBITE:

"Oh, I feel so delightfully white trash! Mummy, I want a mullet!"

Stewie, plucking a banjo.

REVIEW:

"A blend of the ingenious with the raw helps account for its broad appeal – rude, crude and deliciously wrong."

The Seattle Times

Where are those good old fashioned values?

In Quahog, Rhode Island, the Griffins are Peter and Lois, their children Meg, Chris and baby Stewie, and their anthropomorphic talking dog Brian. But you should know that by now. Seth MacFarlane's adult-orientated, animated, black-comedy has been applauded as a pop-culture masterpiece and outrageous satire, as well as having been dismissed as a second-rate rip-off of *The Simpsons*. Filthy, but fiercely smart, the gags fly faster than you can field them, *Family Guy* barges blithely through the barriers of political correctness and declares that absolutely nothing is sacred. Sarah Palin has declared that it is made by "cruel, cold-hearted people".

It's hard to choose the funniest character. Peter is a bumbling slob who makes Homer Simpson seem like a go-getter; the constantly ridiculed Meg is deliciously voiced by Mila Kunis. Stewie is diabolical, a wannabe arch-villain with ambiguous sexual orientation; while Brian the dog, sips martinis, tries to write a novel and hides his love for Lois. Neighbours include Cleveland (who, from 2009, has his own spin-off show), paraplegic cop Joe and depraved Fifties throwback bachelor Quagmire (catchphrase: "*giggity giggity*"). The local news channel is a recurring joke, and any celebrities of the day are deemed fair game for savage, wilfully insensitive take-down. Staunch Democrat MacFarlane, who now hosts Academy Award ceremonies and fills multiplexes with box office hits such as *Ted* and *A Million Ways to Die in the West*, was named Harvard Humanist of the Year in 2011.

If you liked this you'll like:
American Dad!, *The Cleveland Show*, *The Simpsons*.

THE SOPRANOS

CREATED BY:	David Chase
STARRING:	James Gandolfini, Edie Falco, Michael Imperioli, Lorraine Bracco
DATES:	January 1999 – June 2007
SEASONS:	6
EPISODES:	86

SOUNDBITE:

"A wrong decision is better than indecision."

Tony Soprano

REVIEW:

"The richest achievement in the history of television."

The New Yorker

A marriage to the mob, made in Purgatory

"Lately, I'm getting the feeling that I came in at the end", New Jersey mobster Tony Soprano told his psychiatrist. "That the best is over." Yet *The Sopranos*, written by David Chase and others including Matthew Weiner (who went on to create *Mad Men*) and Terence Winter (who created *Boardwalk Empire*), was a beginning. *The Sopranos* wasn't, of course, where great TV began, but it was where a revolution in what could be done within the medium started. With *Oz* having knocked down the jail walls two years earlier, the rulebook was torn up, and the best drama series from here on became braver, darker and brainier as their central characters grew ever more deliciously, intriguingly, infuriatingly complex.

Several templates were set as Tony (the late, great Gandolfini) juggled the conflicting demands of his criminal professional life with his home, family and personal life. The viewer witnessed his everyday existence, which sometimes happened to burst into bouts of graphic violence. A team of crack writers, actors and directors built the show into a filmic equivalent of the fabled Great American Novel, a pop-culture paradigm which resonated as sociology and existentialism while winning 21 Emmys and five Golden Globes. The show asserted the viability of cable and placed HBO in pole position at the start of the twenty-first century. HBO did not let us down. And Chase, he has claimed, had just intended to originally write a show about a man's difficult relationship with his mother. From the off, *The Sopranos* sang a different tune.

If you liked this you'll like:
In Treatment, Magic City, Boardwalk Empire.

THE WEST WING

CREATED BY:	Aaron Sorkin
STARRING:	Martin Sheen, Alison Janney, Richard Schiff, Bradley Whitford
DATES:	September 1999 – May 2006
SEASONS:	7
EPISODES:	156

SOUNDBITE:

"I'm victim to my own purity of character."

President Jed Bartlet

REVIEW:

"A compelling, intelligent and wonderfully engaging drama."

The Hollywood Reporter

Righteous repartee in the White House

"You really felt like you were in the thick of it," said Joss Whedon, a big fan of *The West Wing*. As the men and women of the White House walked-and-talked down the corridors of power, exchanging snappy zingers while trying to do the right and honourable thing, Aaron Sorkin achieved the improbable and made politics hugely entertaining. Sorkin went on to pen Oscar-winning movies such as *The Social Network*, as well as other great TV shows, but the "walk-and-talk" tracking shots co-pioneered with primary director Thomas Schlamme changed the visual vocabulary of drama. Sorkin's scripts, too, made everybody else in network television raise their game, as he fused gravitas with snappy humour.

An idealised Democrat president, Bartlet (Sheen) is flanked by a ensemble of memorable character actors, and deals with scandals, rivalries, shootings, terrorism, campaigns, illness and momentous decisions. Bartlet's senior staff are charming, funny and super smart – the kind of politicos we all wish we had. If *The West Wing* is liberal fantasy, which had sceptics bemoaning its sentimental optimism from the off, its whip-crack wit recalled the heyday of screwball comedy. Few dramas have so righteously revelled in the rhythm and grace of words, while rendering the esoteric electric.

If you liked this you'll like:
Borgen, The Newsroom, House Of Cards.

ANGEL

CREATED BY:	Joss Whedon, David Greenwalt
STARRING:	David Boreanaz, Charisma Carpenter, Amy Acker, Alexis Denisof
DATES:	October 1999 – May 2004
SEASONS:	5
EPISODES:	110

SOUNDBITE:

"You guys go on. I think I'll stay here and not burst into flames."

Angel

REVIEW:

"The LA-set spin-off to *Buffy* was originally dismissed as the original's poor cousin, but gradually developed into a darkly entertaining show in its own right."

The Independent

Buffy's ex goes to hell and back...frequently

Conceived as a murkier, more adult brother to *Buffy*, this stellar spin-off recovered from a shaky start, substituted a character or two, and emerged as a deeply noir, sexy, funny and unique entity. Angel (Boreanaz), Buffy's "ex", is a vampire with a soul – given to him as punishment, it means he is capable of feeling guilt and remorse. Moving to L.A., he sets up as a P.I., aiming to "help the hopeless" with his haphazard team, partly made up of fellow *Buffy* exiles. This being Whedon's world, it's not long before Angel is slaying demons, many of whom run law firm Wolfram & Hart.

The show wasn't afraid of fixing flaws, and grew increasingly gothic (even moving into the Hyperion Hotel to evoke some West Coast history), while turning up the self-aware humour and wise-cracking. By season four, one character complained that he was in "a turgid supernatural soap opera". Support staff Fred, Wesley, Gunn and pacifist-demon and night club crooner Lorne all shine. In season five, Angel is temporarily turned into a puppet: the episode "Smile Time" is genius. And while playing with the genre clichés, Angel still faced urban loneliness, alienation and the spirit of the night, as well as the usual temptations and redemption that face any modern vampire. When the show was prematurely cancelled Whedon was "heartbroken", but, what with *Avengers Assemble* et al, he hasn't done too badly since. *Angel* marks a great talent hitting his groove.

If you liked this you'll like:
Buffy, Firefly, Marvel's Agents Of Shield.

SPACED

CREATED BY:	Simon Pegg, Jessica Stevenson
STARRING:	Simon Pegg, Jessica Stevenson, Nick Frost, Mark Heap
DATES:	September 1999 – April 2001
SEASONS:	2
EPISODES:	14

SOUNDBITE:

"But I hate 'The Time Warp'! It's boil-in-the-bag perversion for sexually repressed accountants and first-year drama students with too many posters of *Betty Blue*, *The Blues Brothers*, *The Big Blue* and *Blue Velvet* on their blue bloody walls!"

Tim

REVIEW:

"Heaps of hilarious pop-culture references… like *Green Card* remade by Quentin Tarantino and Kevin Smith."

Entertainment Weekly

Simon Pegg's sitcom for the jilted generation

Tim and Daisy, twenty-something North Londoners with no clear life plan, pretend to be a "professional couple" (despite barely knowing each other) so they can rent a flat. The building also hosts an eccentric conceptual artist, and friends visit. So far, so typical wacky-young-people sitcom. Then comes the surrealism, and the barrage of knowing, parodic references to cinema from *The Terminator* to *One Flew Over The Cuckoo's Nest*. Among trippy tangents, romantic tensions grow for Tim and Daisy. Pegg pitched the show as "a cross between *The Simpsons*, *The X-Files* and *Northern Exposure*".

With Pegg and Frost now major film stars and director Edgar Wright following the team's trinity of *Shaun Of The Dead*, *Hot Fuzz* and *The World's End* with big-budget Hollywood movies, it's heartening to watch where the group began honing their skills, with outsized ambitions. The international reputation of *Spaced* has snowballed since it emerged blinking and slightly stoned into the world. The 2008 DVD release, for example, featured commentaries from Tarantino, Kevin Smith and *South Park's* Matt Stone. It's a long way from Tufnell Park, where Tim got a letter from his ex-girlfriend full of "you'll always be special" and "I'll always love you platitudes designed to make me feel better while simultaneously appeasing her deep sense of guilt for dumping me and running off with a slimy little city boy called Duane and destroying my faith in everything which is good and pure."

If you liked this you'll like:
Black Books, The Young Ones, Northern Exposure.

THE VICE

CREATED BY:	Barry Simner, Rob Pursey
STARRING:	Ken Stott, Caroline Catz, David Harewood, Rosie Marcel
DATES:	January 1999 – July 2003
SEASONS:	5
EPISODES:	28

SOUNDBITE:

"I've got to hand it to you. I would have just used some tom, but you Pat, you used the woman you love."

DS Vickers

REVIEW:

"A hard-hitting crime drama in which Ken Stott gives a towering performance and dark secrets cause big problems."

Mail Online

Temptation and sin prove utterly gripping

Many (if not all) cop shows are now described as "dark". *The Vice* was ahead of the curve, and perhaps more effective for its relentless negativity and pessimism. Centred (at least until Stott left early in the final season) around a glowering, tortured display of determination and neediness from Stott as DI Pat Chappel, the show dived headlong into the grime and sleaze of London's rapidly-changing Soho. None of its clean-up crusaders could emerge without compromise and guilt.

The Vice Unit is a small but devoted team, led by the obsessive Chappel, whose job is to sweep up the most sordid elements of the criminal underworld (cases involved drugs, prostitution, pornography and paedophilia). Chappel struggles to keep the repulsive world in which he works from infiltrating his lonely home life. He fails, as do most of his colleagues, and lines between right and wrong are frequently, and tragically, fogged, with honey traps and murky deals invariably skewing from the plan. With complex, conflicted roles for Harewood and Catz, both of whom sacrifice almost as much to the job as their boss, and most characters wearing not white or black hats but grey ones, *The Vice* depicts end-of-the-millennium Soho as a microcosm of humankind's fatal flaws. Portishead's "Sour Times" makes for a suitably sad, sinister theme tune.

If you liked this you'll like:
Cracker, Luther, Life On Mars.

CSI: CRIME SCENE INVESTIGATION

CREATED BY:	Anthony E. Zuiker
STARRING:	William Petersen, Marg Helgenberger, Laurence Fishburne, Ted Danson
DATES:	October 2000 – present
SEASONS:	14
EPISODES:	317 (Season 15 imminent, 2014)

SOUNDBITE:

Warrick Brown: "Who brings a gun to a knife fight?"

Gil Grissom: "The winner."

REVIEW:

"The investigations are intriguing. The investigators are blah, their relationships a poorly defined muddle."

Pittsburgh Post-Gazette

The franchise which has longevity in its DNA

A radical howdunnit rather than whodunit, *CSI* was recently named the most watched show in the world. For the fifth time. (The series' worldwide audience in 2009 was estimated as 74 million.) This is a remarkable achievement, despite the show usually focusing on grisly subject matter, and being "unsuitable" for primetime viewing. *CSI* has been slammed for explicit images of violence and sexual fetishism and, in 2005, the episode "King Baby" was cited as "most offensive TV show of the week" by complaining campaigners. And yet *CSI* has survived to the stage of becoming a cosy, familiar institution, spawning spin-offs galore (*CSI: NY*, *CSI: Miami*, and in 2014-15, *CSI: Cyber*) and replacing departing lead actors with barely a blip in those ratings.

So, why has it enjoyed such success? Its "procedural" story-lines are basic, its dialogue functional, its Jerry Bruckheimer production values shiny but uninspired. Forensics, it seems, are the new black. Enamoured of technology, *CSI* offers just enough whizz-bang modernity to enthral and sufficient scientific lingo to give the impression we're learning something. Certainly its inter-cast relationships are lacklustre next to meatier shows. Yet actors as classy as Petersen, Fishburne and Danson have sat in the team-leader seat, suggesting a safe pair of hands at the helm, and Tarantino came on board to direct a special. Interestingly, *CSI* has been credited with raising crime victims' and jurors' expectations of DNA testing to unrealistic levels.

If you liked this you'll like:
Criminal Minds, Without A Trace, CSI: Miami.

CURB YOUR ENTHUSIASM

CREATED BY:	Larry David
STARRING:	Larry David, Jeff Garlin, Cheryl Hines
DATES:	October 2000 – present (eighth season finished in 2011)
SEASONS:	8
EPISODES:	80

SOUNDBITE:

"Pretty good. Pret-tay pret-tay pret-tay good."

Larry

REVIEW:

"As a true 'schlemiel', Larry's failure serves as a direct challenge to the status quo and encourages viewers to question the myriad unwritten rules that we follow in our everyday lives."

David Gillota

Larry David's comedy of errors

One of the most critically acclaimed comedies of the 2000s, *Curb Your Enthusiasm* is more often excruciating than actually funny. David has claimed the title references his perception that people trudge through lives of overt fake optimism: certainly the show takes delight in bursting that bubble. When it opened, the writer-star tried to dampen audience expectations, emphasising that it was no *Seinfeld* (David's previous, hugely popular co-creation). Instead, *Curb Your Enthusiasm* is a semi-improvised, dry, droll and wilfully misanthropic view of modern life, and, like *Seinfeld* before it, struck a chord.

Jerry (Seinfeld) is replaced with Larry, another fictionalised version of the lead, and a semi-retired TV writer-producer. Cheryl, his wife, and Jeff, his manager/confidant, observe aghast as Larry stumbles from social faux pas to fits of irritation, a magnet for awkwardness and embarrassment.

Larry's pettiness, big mouth in small talk, and adherence to strict ethics (except when it suits his own interests) aggravate the itchy tension and collide gauchely with issues like gender and race. For some, *Curb* is miserably unfunny. For many though, it's the most candid, unflinching self-deprecation ever attempted on screen.

If you liked this you'll like:
Louie, The Larry Sanders Show, Bored To Death.

ALIAS

CREATED BY:	J.J. Abrams
STARRING:	Jennifer Garner, Ron Rifkin, Michael Vartan, Bradley Cooper
DATES:	September 2001 – May 2006
SEASONS:	5
EPISODES:	105

SOUNDBITE:

"Some people go miniature-golfing with their parents. We go to India to look for nukes."

Sydney

REVIEW:

"An action-packed weekly adventure that outclassed just about every other show in the genre."

Empire

J.J. Abrams' pre-Lost identity crisis

Sydney Bristow (Garner) is recruited into the CIA fresh from college and drilled in espionage, self-defence and the art of disguise, quickly becoming an international spy. She also moonlights as an agent for criminal organisation Alliance Of Twelve. Her friends and family must never know her true colours, so her adoption of aliases becomes frequent and colourful and allows the show to blend action, intrigue and sci-fi with pithy one-liners and a lot of wigs. *Alias* was the breakthrough Abrams had been waiting for, and who went on to co-create *Lost* and *Fringe*, and not to mention leap into action as the director of both the rebooted *Star Trek* and *Star Wars* franchises.

Alias is a riot of double-crossing and black ops, with themes of loyalty and betrayal – Sydney's father is also a double agent – at its graphic-novel-influenced heart. Midway through Season Two, as we've got to know Sydney's world more, the plot is re-booted and she's allowed a love life of sorts. Later seasons see Sydney suffer trials that would cause Jack Bauer to cuss, while tackling prophecies, pregnancy and the arms trade. With its dash of post-9/11 paranoia, relentless pace and "the most outrageous array of sexy costumes since Cher went off the air," (*USA Today*), *Alias* – never a "major" hit – gained a cult following and threw the spotlight of stardom on Garner, who went on to marry Ben Affleck in 2005, and won a Golden Globe for her role on the show in 2006.

If you liked this you'll like:
Nikita, Dark Angel, Covert Affairs.

THE OFFICE

CREATED BY:	Ricky Gervais, Stephen Merchant
STARRING:	Ricky Gervais, Martin Freeman, Mackenzie Crook, Lucy Davis
DATES:	July 2001 – December 2003
SEASONS:	2
EPISODES:	12 (plus three specials)

SOUNDBITE:

"You just have to accept that some days you are the pigeon, and some days you are the statue."

David Brent

REVIEW:

"As David Letterman keenly observed, this is a series that comes as close to perfect as possible... each episode is genius."

San Francisco Chronicle

Gervais & Merchant's era-defining mockumentary

Almost cancelled early on due to low ratings, *The Office* has now become one of Britain's most successful comedy exports, sold to broadcasters in over eighty countries. The US remake ran for nine seasons. In just two, this no-laugh-track-allowed mockumentary about bored employees and their self-important manager at the Wernham Hogg paper company in Slough, changed the landscape of the comedy of gaucheness and quiet desperation. As *Entertainment Weekly* admitted, "We love the Scranton crew. But the series about the sad-sacks in Slough, England is the undisputed champion of awesomely awkward cubicle hell." It's that pathos-of-the-buffoon thing we Brits do so well – Hancock, Steptoe, Fawlty, Captain Mainwaring, Partridge – that makes these characters internationally popular.

At the show's centre is David Brent (Gervais), "friend and entertainer", who constantly seeks to impress the camera crew and his staff with papier-mache philosophies and misjudged jokes which trip up over unconscious sexism and racism, dovetailing neatly with the idiocy of humourless right-hand man Gareth (Crook). Meanwhile, a star-crossed love story develops between mild-mannered Tim (Freeman) and bored receptionist Dawn (Davis). The two Christmas specials in 2003 conjured up a Hollywood ending which didn't grate, and Brent's hypocrisies and self-promotion have entered the lexicon of business-speak. Brent went on to perform his song "Free Love Freeway" at Wembley Stadium.

If you liked this you'll like:
Extras, Curb Your Enthusiasm, Parks And Recreation.

SIX FEET UNDER

CREATED BY:	Alan Ball
STARRING:	Peter Krause, Michael C. Hall, Frances Conroy, Lauren Ambrose
DATES:	June 2001 – August 2005
SEASONS:	5
EPISODES:	63

SOUNDBITE:

"Isn't it comforting to know that being miserable is still better than being an idiot?"

Claire

REVIEW:

"So daring, richly multi-dimensional and culturally provocative that it's almost anti-television."

The Baltimore Sun

"When death is your business, what is your life?"

American Beauty writer Alan Ball's paradigm-shifting series utilises jet-black comedy to probe the trials and tribulations of the dysfunctional Fisher family, who happen to run a funeral home in L.A. Their lives outside work prove just as challenging as their weekly face-offs with death. From the first scene, the show establishes that it will be unflinching, uncompromising and coruscatingly insightful.

The actors excel too. Krause (whose career has, bizarrely, not taken off since) plays Nate Fisher Jr., who along with his brother David (Hall) is bequeathed the business when his father dies. Both brothers have repressed vulnerabilities; their mother Ruth (Conroy) and sister Claire (Ambrose) are also troubled. Surrealism intrudes, as characters have discussions with the deceased, sometimes while they're being embalmed. Nate's womanising and David's homosexuality lead to primal emotions that often surface at the most inopportune moments. Ball has said that when HBO read his first drafts, they "loved it" but added, "It feels a little safe… could you just make it a little more fucked up?" which, as he remarked, "is not a note you get in Hollywood very often. It gave me free range to go deeper, darker…"

An edgy drama about mortality that's curiously life-affirming, *Six Feet Under* is sometimes icy, sometimes tender, but always implosive.

If you liked this you'll like:
Big Love, The Slap, Nip/Tuck.

BAND OF BROTHERS

PRODUCED BY:	Steven Spielberg, Tom Hanks
STARRING:	Damian Lewis, Ron Livingston, Scott Grimes, Donnie Wahlberg
DATES:	September 2001 – November 2001
SEASONS:	1
EPISODES:	10

SOUNDBITE:

"The only hope you have is to accept the fact you're already dead. The sooner you accept that, the sooner you'll be able to function as a soldier is supposed to function: without mercy, without compassion, without remorse. All war depends upon it."

Ronald Spiers

REVIEW:

"An extraordinary series that balances the ideal of heroism with the violence and terror of battle, reflecting what is both civilised and savage about war."

The New York Times

The realities of war, in all its muddle

Based on Stephen E. Ambrose's novel, *Band Of Brothers*
was backed and urged into being at HBO by Spielberg and
Hanks, after they'd collaborated on the 1998 WWII film
Saving Private Ryan. Based on interviews with veterans, it
dramatises the struggles of "Easy" Company, part of the
101st Airborne Division, from parachute jump training
through battles in Europe until the war's end. It portrays
Major Richard Winters (Lewis) striving to fulfil missions
while keeping his men alive. Somewhat akin to Norman
Mailer's *The Naked And The Dead*, this 10-part, 705-minutes
of epic TV, covers a sprawling ensemble cast but zooms
in on individuals for specific episodes to witness their
participation and reaction to the chaos that surrounds them.
Mentally, physically and morally, they are asked to overcome
horrendous obstacles.

In 2001 *Band Of Brothers* was the most expensive
television mini-series ever made – a cost of $125m – and
remained so until its 2010 sister show, *The Pacific* – and won
six Primetime Emmys. Historical accuracy was considered
paramount by the producers, and most actors spoke with
the veterans they portrayed. Critics acknowledged that it
was "visually astonishing", though some pointed out that
the battle scenes obscured individual characters, making
them difficult to identify. Others argued that this – like
the absence of romances and platitudes, of "narrative
glue" – perfectly represented the fury and muddle of war,
successfully avoiding the traps of cliché.

If you liked this you'll like:
Generation Kill, The Pacific, M*A*S*H.

24

CREATED BY:	Joel Surnow, Robert Cochran
STARRING:	Kiefer Sutherland, Mary Lynn Rajskub, Carlos Bernard, Elisha Cuthbert
DATES:	November 2001 – July 2014
SEASONS:	8 (plus Live Another Day, 2014)
EPISODES:	192 (plus Redemption, 2008)

SOUNDBITE:

"You are going to tell me what I want to know. It's just a matter of how much you want it to hurt."

Jack Bauer

REVIEW:

"An epic poem, with Jack Bauer in the role of Odysseus or Beowulf."

The Los Angeles Times

Jack Bauer's about to have a very bad day. Again

It's easy to underestimate now how radical the approach of 24 was when it made its first impact. Each 24-hour season took us on a day in the frenetic life of CTU (Counter Terrorist Unit) agent Jack Bauer (Sutherland) in "real-time", with a clock ticking. Even as we switched to plot-lines away from the long-suffering Jack, that clock ticked and split-screens shimmered. Jack never had time to sleep, eat, go to the loo, or do anything but save the world, well, mostly, America. Bauer's "ends justify the means" method could be brutal, and it wasn't long before 24 was at the centre of hot debate about US foreign policy, torture techniques and Muslim-phobia. Yet 24 forsake realism early on, throwing itself head-first into one ripping adventure yarn after another with presidential assassination plots, cyber attacks and weapons of mass destruction as nothing but hurdles for the hero to surmount. Bauer, of course, paid the price, but somehow always survived for another adrenalin-charged go-around… 24 is the longest-running spy-themed TV drama ever.

"The role of a lifetime," claimed Sutherland, presumably in a gruff near-whisper. Despite a doomed love-life, a ditzy danger-magnet daughter and a stunning lack of gratitude from those he nominally served, Bauer traversed the sinewy story arcs with craggy conviction. For all the complaints of propaganda and blinkeredness, the exhilarating escapism of 24 remains the box set fans' ultimate box set. Watching just one episode at a time is a mission impossible.

If you liked this you'll like:
Prison Break, Touch, Spooks.

SPOOKS

CREATED BY:	David Wolstencroft
STARRING:	Peter Firth, Matthew Macfadyen, Keeley Hawes, Rupert Penry-Jones
DATES:	May 2002 – October 2011
SEASONS:	10
EPISODES:	88

SOUNDBITE:

"We're in a state of collective desperation here."

Harry Pearce

REVIEW:

"*Spooks* has had a revolving cast since it began, because people are always dying in amazing ways… the plots are like *Dynasty* spliced with *Newsnight*."

The Guardian

British spy series displays its intelligence

Known as *MI-5* in the States, *Spooks* zooms in on the stressful work carried out in the name of British domestic intelligence service. With high production values, labyrinthine plot lines and a surprisingly ruthless willingness to kill off lead characters, it's addictive viewing. You may feel you're learning something about geo-politics and counter-terrorism, but you're not. At the show's heart – like *24*, or *Homeland* – it's a compulsively enjoyable thriller with a generous helping of oh-surely-they-wouldn't-would-they? edge-of-the-seat moments…

Early stars were Macfadyen and Hawes; as the show realized its longevity other spies, not all entirely trustworthy, came in, with the likes of Hermione Norris, Richard Armitage, Miranda Raison and Sophia Myles saving the world and exchanging lingering looks of unresolved sexual attraction. (Then, more often than not, resolving it.) Bombings and killings regularly drew complaints from viewers. Head of the Counter-Terrorism Department, Harry Pearce (Firth) was, seemingly for forever it feels like, put upon and lied to by politicians, anguishing over making the right choices, sacrificing and suffering and ageing into melancholy. A popular export, showing London as shiny and modern and gleaming with iconic landmarks, *Spooks* is powerful, inventive and hard to resist. Harry will be bringing his game back for a forthcoming movie continuation in 2015.

If you liked this you'll like:
Homeland, Line Of Duty, Persons Unknown.

THE WIRE

CREATED BY:	David Simon
STARRING:	Dominic West, Idris Elba, Clarke Peters, Michael K. Williams
DATES:	June 2002 – March 2008
SEASONS:	5
EPISODES:	60

SOUNDBITE:

"All in the game yo, all in the game."

Omar

REVIEW:

"The smartest, deepest and most resonant drama on TV."

Entertainment Weekly

Game on: the show they say is the best ever

Despite only receiving mediocre ratings and few awards, *The Wire* has become recognised as one of the benchmarks of high-quality long-form drama. Its very strengths – multi-layered complexity and gruelling grimness – were perhaps what partitioned it from crossover popularity, but few twenty-first century artworks have enjoyed such a critical consensus. *The Wire* made you work hard and pay attention, but more than rewarded those who did.

Created by former police reporter and author David Simon, it presented a Baltimore riven by desperation and corruption. Each season zoomed in on a different facet of urban decay: the drug trade, the seaport, city politics, the schools, and the print media. An intermingling ensemble of character actors portrayed the ways in which such institutions affected individuals, and how people struggled to survive the trickle-down of trials and vicissitudes. Themes of society and race were sparked into flame by gradually-revealed personalities like detectives Jimmy McNulty (West) and Lester Freamon (Peters), counter-balanced by drug lord Stringer Bell (Elba) and rogue thief Omar (Williams).

Though often compared to "an epic novel", *The Wire* avoided any Dickensian moralising, refusing to serve up catharsis or "just" resolutions. "The game" is what the characters call the drug business, but it fans out without winners, just different shades of loss. Like the reality weathered within *The Wire*, the game grinds on.

If you liked this you'll like:
The Corner, Treme, Southland.

THE SHIELD

CREATED BY:	Shawn Ryan
STARRING:	Michael Chiklis, Glenn Close, Walton Goggins, Catherine Dent
DATES:	March 2002 – November 2008
SEASONS:	7
EPISODES:	88

SOUNDBITE:

"Good cop and bad cop have left for the day. I'm a different kind of cop."

Vic Mackey

REVIEW:

"Detective Vic Mackey didn't just clean up the streets – he cleaned up *on* the streets. Would he pay for those sins? This gutsy drama kept us guessing."

Entertainment Weekly

To protect and to serve?

In an inner city Los Angeles police precinct, some of the cops blur the lines, breaking the law – partly to keep the streets safe, but just as often to serve their self-interests. Alpha male and leader of The Strike Team is Vic Mackey, who with select, trusted friends/colleagues adopts various illegal or unethical methods to lock up bad guys and make personal profit. Planting drugs and forcing confessions are all in a day's work. As the story progresses, the team, increasingly rattled, strive to cover up their crimes, coming under the bright light of scrutiny from crusading "clean" cops. (Great actors like Glenn Close and Forrest Whitaker take a stab at being Mackey's nemesis).

Nervy, claustrophobic and sometimes so tense it feels like there's a grip on your windpipe, *The Shield* has rarely been matched for sheer nail-shredding anxiety. The pit of Purgatory in which Mackey and his gang have landed themselves grows ever more inescapable. Yet they are resourceful, tough, and almost completely devoid of self-doubt. Chiklis' performance as a man whose instincts (he has, of course, some redeeming features) have run amok is one of the most captivating, sustained immersions you'll ever see. *The Shield* is remorseless, brutal and brilliant, and carved "the cop show" a new heart of darkness.

If you liked this you'll like:
The Wire, Southland, Braquo.

NIP/TUCK

CREATED BY:	Ryan Murphy
STARRING:	Dylan Walsh, Julian McMahon, Joely Richardson, Kelly Carlson
DATES:	July 2003 – March 2010
SEASONS:	6
EPISODES:	100

SOUNDBITE:

"Tell me what you don't like about yourself."

Sean & Christian

REVIEW:

"Murphy set out to create a 'deep show about superficiality.' He more than succeeded, and in the process crafted a darkly funny drama about the ugly things people do in the name of beauty."

The Onion A.V. Club

The cut-throat world of modern cosmetic surgery

Nip/Tuck is barking mad, but that's the point. What it *isn't* is just another medical drama. It is hell-bent on going too far. That is it's *modus operandi*. It's *Peyton Place* as made by Federico Fellini. It plunges head-first into hyperbolic, soapy, showboating melodrama, mixing up Douglas Sirk camp and Tarantino pulp, then – and here's the grace note – cartwheels back into genuinely affecting human emotion. An average episode is a riot and a romp, embraces farce and tragedy, froth and misery: and still speaks volumes about the intolerable pressures of modern life.

Sean McNamara (Walsh) and Christian Troy (McMahon) are plastic surgeons, friends/rivals since school, who represent opposing sides of the male ego. Sean is (at first) diffident, submissive, hen-pecked; Christian is an arrogant, narcissistic, sexist hedonist. Each case-of-the-week shows graphic operations, but bounces off the pulsating personal lives of our twin protagonists and their convoluted affairs and crises. After four seasons, now erstwhile celebrities, they relocate from Miami to L.A., but their hilarious-harrowing problems/families/lovers go with them. Sean often bails out Christian's botch-ups, but his patience is wearing…

Over one hundred episodes the volume is turned up louder and louder, with the twists and shocks and committed (yet winking-and-nudging) performances soaring beyond implausible into the sleazily operatic. Murphy's next trick was *Glee*, but *Nip/Tuck* is where he gleefully gets away with murder, sex and laying bare the male psyche.

If you liked this you'll like:
Six Feet Under, House Of Cards, Californication.

PEEP SHOW

CREATED BY:	Andrew O'Connor, Jesse Armstrong, Sam Bain
STARRING:	David Mitchell, Robert Webb, Matt King, Olivia Colman
DATES:	September 2003 – present
SEASONS:	8 (Season 9 films in 2015)
EPISODES:	48

SOUNDBITE:

"She's so beautiful and fancy. If there weren't a junkie in my room shitting and retching and hurling, it'd be just like *Pride And Prejudice*."

Jeremy

REVIEW:

"In years to come *Peep Show* will be seen as the pinnacle of comedy it obviously is."

Daily Mirror

Sitcom looks at "London losers" from acute angles

The enduring *Peep Show*, a curious Frankenstein's monster fusion of *The Likely Lads*, *Men Behaving Badly*, *Being John Malkovich* and *Annie Hall*, has never boasted large TV viewing figures but has proven a sleeper hit through high DVD sales. The POV filming style – used less and less in later series – has alienated the mainstream, according to producer O'Connor. Nonetheless, it's won everything from the Rose D'Or to Baftas, and its originality and freshness – and near-the-knuckle candour concerning the psyches of frustrated men – have earned it a loyal cult following. It's the longest returning comedy in Channel 4's history.

The contrasting, yet mutually dependent pair who slump from dissatisfied twenty-somethings to desperate thirty-somethings, Mark (Mitchell) and Jeremy (Webb) share a flat in Croydon. Mark is, in the main, gainfully employed and responsible, while Jez is a would-be"boho"wannabe-musician. Mark is buttoned-up and socially awkward; Jez is misguidedly cocky, optimistic and shameless. Each craves more success with women than they have, generally flailing in a puddle of inappropriate narcissism and all the while relaying to us, in voiceover, their most embarrassing confessional thoughts. They need to get as far away from each other's influence and emotional blackmail as possible but, like *Steptoe & Son*, or post-lad-mag Pinter characters, are forever doomed to detrimental symbiosis.

If you liked this you'll like:
Fresh Meat, *That Mitchell And Webb Look*, *The Young Ones*.

ARRESTED DEVELOPMENT

CREATED BY:	Mitchell Hurwitz
STARRING:	Jason Bateman, Portia De Rossi, Will Arnett, Michael Cera, Tony Hale
DATES:	November 2003 – February 2006, revived May 2013
SEASONS:	4
EPISODES:	68

SOUNDBITE:

"You should have seen the face he made when…. well he's my twin brother, I'll show you."

George Bluth

REVIEW:

"Here to save the day… a farce of such blazing wit and originality that it must surely usher in a new era in comedy."

The Guardian

The story of a wealthy family who lost everything...

When his once-wealthy father is imprisoned, level-headed
Michael Bluth (Bateman) steps in to take care of family
affairs. He's underestimated the antics of his dysfunctional,
selfish relatives, who make his task highly challenging.
Michael – a widowed single dad and the show's straight
man, for all Bateman's wonderful reaction shots – strives
to do the right thing while the others engage in gross
materialism, greed, incestuous undertones, hedonism and
chronic manipulation. His son, George Michael (Cera),
feels the burden of the pressure to be as decent as his dad,
while Michael's father (Jeffrey Tambor, once Hank in *The
Larry Sanders Show*) is an amoral control freak. Mother
Lucille is permanently drunk, her youngest son Buster is
prone to panic attacks, her oldest, Gob, is a failed magician.
Daughter Lindsay is spoiled; her husband Tobias Funke is
a psychiatrist-turned-actor. Got that? If not, narrator Ron
Howard will guide you through, albeit wilfully imperfectly.

It was director Howard who initially wanted to make
a comedy series in the fashion of reality TV, with handheld
cameras. Hurwitz suggested the "riches to rags" Californian
family set-up: a bidding war between Fox and NBC ensued.
Fox won, but though acclaim poured in, ratings didn't. Upon
cancellation, however, the show's web-wide cult following
raised their voices for years until Netflix eventually stepped
in. A speedy, delirious gag-fest, revelling in absurdity.

If you liked this you'll like:
Soap, Modern Family, Community.

LOST

CREATED BY:	Jeffrey Lieber, J.J. Abrams, Damon Lindelof
STARRING:	Matthew Fox, Evangeline Lily, Jorge García, Michelle Rodriguez
DATES:	September 2004 – May 2010
SEASONS:	6
EPISODES:	121

SOUNDBITE:

"If I don't play ping-pong every 108 minutes the whole island's gonna explode."

Sawyer

REVIEW:

"*Lost* has maximised the potential of narrative uncertainty and made it a beguiling constant."

The New York Times

Lost? Exactly how you'll feel when it's all over

Lost is regularly listed among the best cult shows of all time, but most commentaries both praise its neo-mystical beginnings and damn its botched denouement. Upon arrival, it was celebrated for its mix of humanistic worldview and cryptic, wilfully incongruous symbolism, which had fans heatedly debating the *meaning* of it all. What was going on on that island? As seasons drifted by, for many it disappeared up its own mythology and dropped into a finale which one critic dismissed as "poppycock". Others considered it spiritual and moving. As *Entertainment Weekly* put it: "Plane crash. Smoke monster. Polar bear. Crazy French lady. The Others. The hatch. The Dharma Initiative. Time-travel flashes. Name another network drama that can so wondrously turn a question mark into an exclamation mark."

Stirring up sci-fi, the supernatural and *Lord Of The Flies*, *Lost* made the name of J.J. Abrams, though, in fact, after the pilot it was Lieber and Lindelof who were show-runners and head writers. As the survivors of a plane crash on a tropical island experienced bewilderment, angst and flashbacks (telling us their back stories), a fictional universe was created which encouraged in fans the joys and frustrations of guesswork. It surprised, it stuttered, it revived and, in the end, told us to keep on guessing.

If you liked this you'll like:
Heroes, Fringe, Alias

DEADWOOD

CREATED BY:	David Milch
STARRING:	Timothy Olyphant, Ian McShane, Molly Parker, Powers Boothe
DATES:	March 2004 – August 2006
SEASONS:	3
EPISODES:	36

SOUNDBITE:

"Pain or damage don't end the world. Or despair or fucking beatings. The world ends when you're dead. Until then, you got more punishment in store. Stand it like a man. And give some back."

Al Swearengen

REVIEW:

"A brilliant allegory for the evolution of American capitalism."

Time Out New York

The wild, wild West – with strong, strong language

"The Holy Trinity of HBO dramas", writer Alan Sepinwall
has observed, "were created by men called David". Chase
gave us *The Sopranos* in 2002, Simon *The Wire* in 2002, and
Milch *Deadwood* two years later. Milch had paid his dues
on the brilliant *NYPD Blue*, but when liberated from any
network niceties he threw away all filters and came up with
a Western series like none that had gone before.

In corrupt, lawless 1870s South Dakota, Deadwood
grows from small sub-town to proto-capitalist community.
Some characters (Wild Bill Hickok, Wyatt Earp, Calamity
Jane) and events are based on recorded history. Others
aren't. The ingenious, robust obscenity and swearing is the
author's own. *Deadwood* won plentiful awards and is often
cited as a classic case of a show being cancelled prematurely.

Brothel-owner Al Swearengen (British veteran McShane
in a career-refuelling role) and sheriff Seth Bullock
(Olyphant) were the nominal leads, but *Deadwood* boasted a
rich ensemble with almost every role granted ripe dialogue.
McShane was only offered the role after Powers Boothe, cast
in the role, fell ill (Milch wrote Boothe the part of Cy Tolliver
as solace). And Swearengen gradually evolved from villain to
unorthodox hero, much as a previous Milch creation, Dennis
Franz's Andy Sipowicz, had in *NYPD Blue*. Milch's great
talent – and some might say HBO's – was to draw viewers in
with sexy-dirty material, then hit them with the big themes
and the hard stuff. *Deadwood* was a new kind of realism.

If you liked this you'll like:
Justified, Boardwalk Empire, Sons Of Anarchy.

THE L WORD

CREATED BY:	Ilene Chaiken, Michele Abbot, Kathy Greenberg
STARRING:	Jennifer Beals, Mia Kirshner, Erin Daniels, Pam Grier
DATES:	January 2004 – March 2009
SEASONS:	6
EPISODES:	70

SOUNDBITE:

"If you think men are the enemy, then you and I are going to have a serious problem."

Moira Sweeney

REVIEW:

"Before *The L Word*, lesbian characters barely existed in television. Showtime's decision to air *The L Word* was akin to ending a drought with a monsoon."

The New York Times

Pioneering, if glossed, lesbian romance

The *L Word*, set in West Hollywood, follows the lives and loves of a close-knit group of lesbians and bisexuals and their friends and families – supportive or otherwise. The working code title for the project was "Earthlings" (an infrequently encountered slang term for lesbians). So complex was the show's web of relationships that lead character, Alice, had "The Chart" tattooed onto her back as a semi-comic device.

Reaction to the show was split. For every critic who acclaimed the show's bravery and frankness in standing up to the religious Right, there was another who deplored its unrealistic glamour and "Sapphic *Playboy* fantasia". For some, it was just an edgier *Sex and the City*. All, however, agreed that the show broke new ground. It wasn't prudish, and its ensemble spanned diverse story strains. Central were Bette (Beals, a long way from *Flashdance* and maturing into a nicely nuanced actor) and Tina (Laurel Holloman), a couple, trying to have a baby. New neighbour Jenny (Kirshner) starts the sub-plots rolling in the deep that's just under the glossy surface of their hip zip code. And for all its slick top layer of crossover-audience seduction, *The L Word*, while luxuriant and licentious, often cuts to the bone of love, loyalty and longing.

If you liked this you'll like:
Queer As Folk, Sugar Rush, Gossip Girl.

BATTLESTAR GALACTICA

DEVELOPED BY:	Ronald D. Moore (based on the Glen A. Larson series)
STARRING:	Edward James Olmos, Mary McDonnell, Katee Sackhoff, Jamie Bamber
DATES:	October 2004 – March 2009
SEASONS:	4
EPISODES:	75

SOUNDBITE:

"Love is a strange and wonderful thing, chief. You be happy you experienced it at all… even if it was with a machine."

Dr Gaius Baltar

REVIEW:

"Look at this saga any way you want – as political drama, religious debate, psychological suspense, sci-fi adventure, deep metaphor or just plain fun – and it's scintillating from every angle."

Newsday

Stunning space opera offering sci-fi for grown-ups

Pushed for the greatest TV series ever made, many will cite *Breaking Bad*, *The Wire*, *The Sopranos* or *Mad Men*. Yet away from the consensus, you'll find a growing, savvy contingent who got past the starting point that this *Battlestar Galactica* was a radical re-imagining of a trashy 1970s sci-fi throwaway and found that it created an immersive universe of its own, peopling it with complex, compelling characters, profound allegory, violence, rage, lust and turmoil. The show is, easily, the darkest space opera America has produced: It took huge risks and delivered a richly rewarding, thought-provoking human drama, transcending any genre.

On a distant star system, humans survive on a group of planets known as The Twelve Colonies. The Cylons – cybernetic human creations – wage war, leaving only fifty thousand humans alive. In deep space, a military starship, *Battlestar Galactica*, takes on the challenge of leading the fugitives to fabled refuge "Earth".

This premise doesn't do it justice: *BSG* examines theology, polytheism, fundamentalism and – symbolically – terrorism. With fierce feminism it covers sex, despair, identity and moral grey areas. There are episodes which hum with tension (part *The West Wing*, part *Blade Runner*) and story-arc revelations that pull the rug from under you. Who *are* the Final Five? The show's ending infuriated as many as it gratified. A long, long way from the *USS Enterprise*, *Battlestar Galactica* is adult, apocalyptic and in every way awesome.

If you liked this you'll like:
Caprica, Star Trek, Deadwood.

ENTOURAGE

CREATED BY:	Doug Ellin
STARRING:	Adrian Grenier, Kevin Dillon, Jeremy Piven, Kevin Connolly
DATES:	July 2004 – September 2011
SEASONS:	8
EPISODES:	96

SOUNDBITE:

"We are gonna get drunk with Russell Crowe and we are gonna head-butt some goddam kangaroos."

Ari Gold

REVIEW:

"Almost always smart, sharp and funny."

Wall Street Journal

Every male's favourite envy-watch

Mark Wahlberg, executive-producer, says the premise of
Entourage is based on his own experiences as an up-and-
coming movie star. (Originally a documentary was mooted).
It chronicles the Hollywood acting career and love life of
Vincent Chase (Grenier), who's supported by his gang of
childhood friends from Queens, New York – a wannabe
nu-school Rat Pack – as they conquer L.A. Unabashedly
celebrating male bonding, the show is a magnet to famous
guests (from Martin Scorsese and Dennis Hopper to
Eminem and Kanye West), seeking to wink to us that they
too grasp fully the craziness and shallowness of Tinseltown.
The comedy-drama sometimes seems to be a homage to
screenwriter William Goldman's renowned dictum: Nobody
Knows Anything. Not that Vincent's complaining (much), as
A-list stardom comes his way.

Vinnie's best friend is Eric (Connolly), his manager,
while his older half-brother Johnny "Drama" (Dillon) is his
chef/trainer/bodyguard, and a frustrated C-lister himself.
Turtle is his "gofer". There is an endless parade of glamorous
girlfriends. However, the show is stolen by the louder-than-
life performance of Piven as agent Ari Gold. His colourful
language and remorseless powers of persuasion are the
licentious lifeblood of the series, which is male fantasy
fulfilment writ large but also a paean to friendship. A film,
doubtless cameo-packed, is on the way in summer 2015.

If you liked this you'll like:
Californication, Hung, Shameless.

HOUSE M.D.

CREATED BY:	David Shore
STARRING:	Hugh Laurie, Omar Epps, Robert Sean Leonard, Olivia Wilde, Lisa Edelstein, Jennifer Morrison, Jesse Spencer
DATES:	November 2004 – May 2012
SEASONS:	8
EPISODES:	177

SOUNDBITE:

"A unicorn isn't a unicorn. It's a donkey with a plunger stuck to its face."

Dr Gregory House

REVIEW:

"An uncommon cure for the common medical drama."

TV Guide

Unexpected reinvention: A Laurie-load of surprises

Described as "the most electrifying new main character to hit television in years", *House M.D.* made an unlikely international star of British comic-fop actor Hugh Laurie, previously best known for clattering around gamely with Stephen Fry and in *Blackadder*. His reinvention as the maverick, antisocial, unsympathetic doctor, on a show which took up residency in the US top ten, won him two Golden Globes and a newly flourishing career.

Shore had worked as a writer on *Due South* and a producer on *NYPD Blue* when he was asked to fuse a police procedural with a medical drama. Shore, inspired by *Sherlock Holmes*, pushed for the idea of the mystery being less important and interesting than the hero. Thus came House, flouting the rules, often in conflict with the bosses, diagnosing the undiagnosable. His injured leg – exacerbated by an incorrect diagnosis – gives him an addiction to painkillers and a degree in grumpy. The more baffling the case, the greater the wit and flash of curveball inspiration with which House and his crack team of doctors (played by a first-rate ensemble) will solve it.

House M.D. was hailed as both a "nasty" black comedy and "satisfying and basic medical TV". As seasons developed, so did the unorthodox mix of misery, dysfunctional relationships and shrewd humour.

If you liked this you'll like:
*Sherlock, ER, M*A*S*H.*

WEEDS

CREATED BY:	Jenji Kohan
STARRING:	Mary-Louise Parker, Elizabeth Perkins, Justin Kirk, Kevin Nealon
DATES:	August 2005 – September 2012
SEASONS:	8
EPISODES:	102

SOUNDBITE:

"It's a weed wonderland, Nancy. It's like Amsterdam only you don't have to visit the Anne Frank house and pretend to be all sad and shit."

Doug Wilson

REVIEW:

"Each episode contains hilarious lines but no laugh track, offering a light touch on a cross-section of heavy issues: drugs, race, illness and sex."

The Guardian

Mary-Louise Parker breaks bad...

A "dramedy" from the same Showtime stable as
Californication and *Nurse Jackie*, *Weeds* brought a Golden
Globe to the perennially underrated Mary-Louise Parker
who is in her whip-smart element here as Nancy Botwin,
a Southern California housewife who uses her initiative to
become a pot dealer after her husband dies. At first sneered
at by neighbours, although her activities support her family,
her success grows to international cartel levels, via three
marriages and jail time. Sound familiar in some ways? *Weeds*
preceded *Breaking Bad*. And has loads more jokes.

Kohan, who went on to create *Orange Is The New Black*,
claims the title refers both to cannabis and widow's weeds as
well as "hardy plants struggling to survive". The supporting
cast display twists on the obligatory colourful and eccentric:
Weeds is both risqué and robust, as dark as it is goofy.
Martin Donovan, Matthew Modine and Richard Dreyfuss
are among Nancy's imperfect suitors, but the series is also
exemplary in providing rich roles to women in their forties,
with Perkins showboating magnificently. All this plus Alanis
Morissette, Zooey Deschanel, Carrie Fisher, and one Snoop
Dogg, offering up a respectful rap to Nancy's "milf weed".
Weeds works on a number of high levels.

If you liked this you'll like:
Orange Is The New Black, Nurse Jackie, Breaking Bad.

THE OFFICE: AN AMERICAN WORKPLACE

DEVELOPED BY:	Greg Daniels (based on the UK series by Ricky Gervais and Stephen Merchant)
STARRING:	Steve Carell, Rainn Wilson, John Krasinski, Jenna Fischer
DATES:	March 2005 – May 2013
SEASONS:	9
EPISODES:	201

SOUNDBITE:

"Do I want to be feared or loved? That's a good question. I want both. I want people to be afraid of how much they love me."

Michael Scott

REVIEW:

"This undervalued remake does the near-impossible – it honours the original and works on its own terms."

Entertainment Weekly

Mr Brent Goes to Pennsylvania

History is littered with the debris of US remakes of UK comedy hits, which seemed like a good idea at the time but failed dismally to translate, hitting cancellation almost before the opening credits had rolled. *Fawlty Towers* (in three different guises), *Absolutely Fabulous*, *Red Dwarf*, *Coupling*, and *The Inbetweeners* have all bombed there, often at the pilot stage. *The Office* however moved from Slough, Berkshire to Scranton, Pennsylvania with all-round success, bagging four Primetime Emmys and – after a shaky first season – becoming so popular that in 2009 it was scheduled to follow the Superbowl.

Credit for making Ricky Gervais an even richer man must be shared between the adaptation skills of veteran *Saturday Night Live/The Simpsons* writer Greg Daniels, Steve Carell's fearlessly self-effacing comedy chops and the timing and judgment of a strong supporting cast. As time went by it developed its own identity (with a magnificent spin on the Tim-Dawn love story subplot played out by Krasinski and Fischer) and critics claimed its quality surpassed the original source. Will Ferrell and James Spader featured in later seasons, while Mindy Kaling went on to create the similarly-toned *The Mindy Project*. To quote Carell's Scott – the American David Brent – "Let them eat cake. Margaret Thatcher said that about marriage. Smart broad."

If you liked this you'll like:
The Office, Parks And Recreation, The Mindy Project.

PRISON BREAK

CREATED BY:	Paul Scheuring
STARRING:	Wentworth Miller, Dominic Purcell, Robin Tunney, Peter Stormare
DATES:	August 2005 — May 2009
SEASONS:	4
EPISODES:	81

SOUNDBITE:

"This is going wrong in every possible way…"

Michael Scofield

REVIEW:

"Rocking good entertainment… taut, ingenious story-telling."

Detroit Free Press

The almost-great escape...

On its debut, *Prison Break* pulled in numbers Fox hadn't
seen in that slot since *Melrose Place* and *Ally McBeal*. For a
time it drew both glowing reviews and big audiences. Then:
the decline. Later in its four-year run, former fans were
bemoaning its "overwrought performances" and "lazy" plot
fixes, and its ultimate demise went largely unmourned. It
failed to break out of its blockage. But for a while there, its
simple but wonderfully insane premise had millions hooked.

One brother has been sentenced to death for a crime
– the murder of the Vice President's brother – that he
didn't commit. The other (Miller, briefly a heartthrob and
the Golden Globe-nominated talk of town during the
first season; now a successful screenwriter) conceives an
elaborate plan to get him out of jail. It's quite a plan: he
commits armed robbery to get into the same penitentiary,
where he works on befriending the influential. Tattoos are
involved, as is some macho posturing. Season Two moves
things outward and has been compared to *The Great Escape*
and *The Fugitive*, which makes you wonder what they do
with the next two seasons, so, suffice to say, there are twists.
Some clever, some dumb. As ratings decreased, Fox's Kevin
Reilly admitted, "The show has just played out."

If you liked this you'll like:
24, Oz, Sons Of Anarchy.

EXTRAS

CREATED BY:	Ricky Gervais, Stephen Merchant
STARRING:	Ricky Gervais, Ashley Jensen, Stephen Merchant, Shaun Williamson
DATES:	July 2005 – December 2007
SEASONS:	2
EPISODES:	13 (Includes Christmas Special)

SOUNDBITE:

Patrick Stewart: "You're not married, you haven't got a girlfriend, and you don't watch *Star Trek*?"

Andy: "No."

Patrick Stewart: "Good Lord."

REVIEW:

"As hilarious and heartbreaking as *The Office*."

Matt Groening

Gervais and Merchant take down fame.

Andy Millman (Gervais) is a struggling, bitter actor, Darren Lamb (Merchant) is his useless apathetic agent and Maggie (Jensen) is Millman's fuzzy-headed but loyal friend. Andy pins his hopes of fame on his sitcom script. By season two, the sitcom has become a popular BBC show but Andy, ego raging, has not won any kudos. In the Christmas Special wrap-up, he is infuriated by the chasm between success and respect, while Maggie, still struggling to land roles, finds his constant discontent baffling.

After *The Office*, Gervais and Merchant were such hot property that HBO and BBC co-produced *Extras*. Celebs queued up to send themselves up in unflattering roles while, of course, signalling that they were good sports. Hollywood A-listers like Kate Winslet, Ben Stiller, Samuel L. Jackson, Daniel Radcliffe and even Robert De Niro took part, while the use of Les Dennis and Keith Chegwin riffed sharply on the diverse levels (or circles of hell) of "fame". The more Andy realizes his fantasies of glory, the more disappointed he is. David Bowie's cameo, serenading him with "Little Fat Man" is his defining moment – until that finale, wherein he explodes, rails at modern celebrity (while in the *Celebrity Big Brother* house), and grasps the redemption of friendship.

It's easy now, with the opprobrium hurled at his later work, to forget how hard-hitting and perceptive Gervais' greatest piece was. *Extras* is fearless, funny and astute.

If you liked this you'll like:
The Larry Sanders Show, Entourage, Rev.

GREY'S ANATOMY

CREATED BY:	Shonda Rhimes
STARRING:	Ellen Pompeo, Sandra Oh, Katherine Heigl, Patrick Dempsey
DATES:	March 2005 – present
SEASONS:	11
EPISODES:	220 (ongoing)

SOUNDBITE:

"We're adults. When did that happen? And how do we make it stop?"

Dr Meredith Grey

REVIEW:

"Expertly weaves its signature elements of complex relationships, whimsical banter and challenging life-lessons, all to a montage-fetish, indie-rock soundtrack."

IGN

Doctors and nurses with added indie anthems

Following the lives at work and play of good-looking interns at a Seattle hospital as they graduate into experienced doctors, *Grey's Anatomy* has often been accused of mimicking *ER*. It has enjoyed that show's longevity, and its popularity, while declining in recent years, has been major-league.

With its title an awkward play on Henry Gray's anatomy textbook, its central role is taken by Dr Meredith Grey (Pompeo), though one of the show's most commendable, appealing features has been its racially diverse cast. Creator Rhimes (now working on *Scandal*) has said she craved a show about"smart women competing against each other", but it's hardly as cut-throat as that sounds. Asked how it differed from the likes of *ER*, ABC remarked that while everyone else was speeding up their medical dramas, Rhimes"found a way to slow it down, so you get to know the characters. There's definitely a strong female appeal to it."

Even those involved did not expect the series to take off to the extent it has. As seasons flew by, the actors' chemistry was praised but plots were accused of predictability. Meredith moved from romantic dilemmas to what were dubbed"soliloquys"about Patrick Dempsey's"McDreamy". A spin-off, *Private Practice*, ran for six seasons, starring Kate Walsh. Pompeo and Heigl both openly expressed their displeasure that that gig wasn't theirs.

If you liked this you'll like:
ER, Scrubs, Private Practice.

THE THICK OF IT

CREATED BY:	Armando Iannucci
STARRING:	Peter Capaldi, Chris Addison, Rebecca Front, James Smith.
DATES:	May 2005 – October 2012
SEASONS:	4.
EPISODES:	24.

SOUNDBITE:

"You don't seem to understand that I'm going to have to mop up a f**ing hurricane of piss from all these neurotics."

Malcolm Tucker

REVIEW:

"Political comedy The Thick Of It may be satire, but many of its storylines have apparently come to life. What does this tell us about modern politics?"

BBC News

Political satire taken to the extreme

"*Yes Minister* meets Larry Sanders", Armando Iannucci has said, though its profanity count sends it careening away from such relatively modest ambitions into a parental-advisory parenthesis. A savage, scabrous, stabilisers-off satire of the corridors of power and spin which constitute the modern British government, *The Thick Of It* rams home the truth that the twenty-first century would appear alien terrain to the gentlemen of Jay and Lynn's 1980s sitcom. A film spin-off, *In The Loop*, proved that it was – against all odds – possible to take things further, and while a US remake stalled, much of the same team's *Veep* (starring Seinfeld's Julia Louis-Dreyfus as the US VP) has been hailed as "hysterical".

Hysteria abounds – both as farce and blind panic – as the hard-to-ignore Malcolm Tucker (Capaldi), Number 10's indomitably fierce and aggressive "enforcer", keeps a watchful eye on ministers and underlings. His radiantly colourful use of language has a cult following of its own. Although political parties aren't mentioned by name, context tips us the wink as to what we're witnessing. So influential did the show's caustic commentaries become that the word "omnishambles", coined in the third series, entered House of Commons discourse, with Labour leader Ed Miliband, in a case of near-life imitating art, subsequently tossing it at the Tories.

If you liked this you'll like:
2012, Yes Minister, Veep.

30 ROCK

CREATED BY:	Tina Fey
STARRING:	Tina Fey, Alec Baldwin, Jane Krakowski, Tracy Morgan
DATES:	October 2006 – January 2013
SEASONS:	7
EPISODES:	138

SOUNDBITE:

Jack: "Lemon, I'm impressed. You're starting to think like a businessman."
Liz Lemon: "A businesswoman."
Jack: "I don't think that's a word."

REVIEW:

"Like the best comedies – from *Seinfeld* to *Mary Tyler Moore* to *Jack Benny* – 30 Rock sparkles not just because its central star gets to shine, but because everyone does."

The New York Daily News

Tina Fey's meta-sitcom. Alec Baldwin's finest hour

At NBC's 30 Rockefeller Plaza Studio, sketch-show head writer Liz Lemon (Fey) finds the tastes of new boss Jack Donaghy (Baldwin) demanding and sometimes demeaning. Her none-more-blonde friend Jenna (Krakowski) is clinging on to her star status while volatile comedian Tracy Jordan (Morgan) is Donaghy's preference. As the seasons solidify, plots revolve less around the TV show and instead tickle the cast's (usually disastrous) personal lives and relationships.

The glory of *30 Rock*, loosely based on Fey's experiences at *Saturday Night Live*, is its rapid-fire pace. Though it didn't go short of awards, it struggled somewhat for viewers, despite celebrity cameos from Steve Martin, Jennifer Aniston, Matt Damon, Julianne Moore, LL Cool J and Jon Bon Jovi, to name but a few. There was, at first, some perceived competition with the similarly-set Aaron Sorkin drama *Studio 60 on the Sunset Strip*, but – as the NBC President pointed out – there were invariably more than one cop or hospital show in the listings. *30 Rock* grabs you by the collar and races you breathlessly through zinger after zinger, Fey's quicksilver writing (as showcased in the classic *Mean Girls*) at its immaculate finest.

If you liked this you'll like:
Parks And Recreation, Brooklyn Nine-Nine, The Mindy Project.

DEXTER

DEVELOPED BY:	James Manos Jr
STARRING:	Michael C. Hall, Jennifer Carpenter, Julie Benz, Desmond Harrington
DATES:	October 2006 – September 2013
SEASONS:	8
EPISODES:	96

SOUNDBITE:

"I've lived in darkness a long time. Over the years my eyes adjusted, until the dark became my world and I could see."

Dexter

REVIEW:

"*Dexter* is yet another temptation that is almost impossible to resist."

The New York Times

American Psycho turns vicious vigilante

Controversial from debut to finale, *Dexter* gave us a new kind of serial killer, an anti-hero who works as a blood spatter analyst for the Miami police. In his downtime he hunts criminals who have slipped the net of legal justice, and exacts merciless, macabre punishment.

Orphaned at three and adopted, Dexter was taught by his cop father to only let his homicidal impulses out on the most heinous and deserving. He must keep up appearances as a "normal" member of society, but his bloodlust is unremitting. Dexter retains a morsel of our sympathy through "everyday" personal relationship issues and the curiously magnetic performance of Michael C. Hall, who had previously wowed in *Six Feet Under*.

As *Dexter* became a surprisingly durable hit despite much criticism for its amorality and graphic violence, guest stars from John Lithgow and Jimmy Smits to Julia Stiles and Charlotte Rampling lined up to revel in the repulsion. (Hall and Lithgow won Golden Globes in 2010). In America, copycat killers compared themselves to the show's Patrick Bateman-esque lead and politicians complained about scenes of sex and dismemberment. Yet Dexter kept his hold on our imagination, partly through his wry, ever-present voice-over: "I'm a very neat monster".

If you liked this you'll like:
Bates Motel, American Horror Story, Six Feet Under.

LIFE ON MARS

CREATED BY:	Matthew Graham, Tony Jordan, Ashley Pharoah
STARRING:	John Simm, Philip Glenister, Liz White, Dean Andrews
DATES:	January 2006 – April 2007
SEASONS:	2
EPISODES:	16

SOUNDBITE:

"There will never be a woman prime minister as long as I have a hole in my arse."

Gene Hunt

REVIEW:

"As poor Sam Tyler walks through his sunken dream, we're hooked to the silver screen."

The Guardian

Oh man, look at those (Seventies) cavemen go...

This recipe of nostalgia and knowingness lets us have our cake and eat it. As *The Telegraph* wrote, "Theoretically, this should add up to a right old mess. In practice, it makes for thumpingly enjoyable television." Its curious conceit – time-warp police procedural spliced with giddying science fiction – arguably didn't sustain for two series, but the love-hate chemistry of its two leads and its juxtaposition of period attitudes were the hotly-discussed topics of its time(s).

The premise, spinning tangentially off a Bowie lyric, is bananas. Simm's DCI Sam Tyler wakes from a 2006 car accident to find himself in 1973 Manchester: era of flares, Ford Cortinas and since-discredited police methodology. There's also his boss, Gene Hunt (Glenister), a Jack Regan (from *The Sweeney*) type who Sam considers an "overweight, over-the-hill, nicotine-stained, borderline alcoholic homophobe with a superiority complex and an unhealthy obsession with male bonding". He's just one of Sam's problems, what with not knowing if he's in a coma or if Hunt and the rest of this world are a figment of his imagination. The series' popularity led to a three-season sequel, *Ashes To Ashes*, pitching Keeley Hawes with/against Gene in the 1980s. Both shows boasted killer pop soundtracks, while *Life On Mars* spawned a short-lived US remake starring Harvey Keitel as Hunt. There was even a Russian adaptation, *The Dark Side Of The Moon*.

If you liked this you'll like:
Ashes To Ashes, Life On Mars (US), The Sweeney.

SKINS

CREATED BY:	Bryan Elsley, Jamie Brittain
STARRING:	Nicholas Hoult, Dev Patel, Kaya Scodelario, Jack O'Connell, Freya Mavor
DATES:	January 2007 – August 2013
SEASONS:	7
EPISODES:	61

SOUNDBITE:

"Love, love, love… what is it good for? Absolutely nothing."

Effy Stonem

REVIEW:

"It really doesn't care how much it hacks parents off… what's striking is the absolute inadequacy of every single adult character, their complete subordination to comic business."

The Independent

Whatever happened to the teenage dream?

Nominally a "teen drama" immersing itself in the lives and loves of a group of Bristol sixth formers, *Skins* (named after rolling papers) laced its titillating hedonism with scenes and twists of extraordinary pathos and insight. Over its six years, it mixed the surface glamour of beautiful people partying with acute storylines exploring mental illness, sexual identity, drug abuse and bullying. It did this without ever condescending, patronising or lecturing. *Skins* is both the wild up-all-night rock 'n' roll ride of laughs and lust it was first pitched as and a cool, unblinking commentary on the same. It also boasts love stories that seem more inspired by Stendhal or Rohmer than *Grange Hill*. An American remake was ditched after one season as conservative advertisers found it too unhinged and controversial.

The British template however kept on regenerating. Atypically, it culled its lead cast every two seasons, bringing in fresh faces with new issues. This was no problem for several actors, who went on to huge Hollywood success (e.g. Hoult, Patel). Among the many stand-out characters were Cook (O'Connell) and Effy (Scodelario), the latter – an enigmatic, fearless muse and leader – perhaps the series' fulcrum. Guesting as obtuse parents were everyone from Peter Capaldi to Harry Enfield to Bill Bailey. High and heightened, *Skins* tackles its matters of life and death with light and depth.

If you liked this you'll like:
Freaks And Geeks, Fresh Meat, My Mad Fat Diary.

THE KILLING

CREATED BY:	Søren Sveistrup
STARRING:	Sofie Gråbøl, Søren Malling, Morten Suurballe, Mikael Birkkjær, Nikolaj Lie Kaas
DATES:	January 2007 – November 2012
SEASONS:	3
EPISODES:	40

SOUNDBITE:

"You know full well that when it comes to feelings, you tend to run away…"

Mathias Borch to Sarah Lund

REVIEW:

"A remarkable piece of television. Its sheer narrative ambition is unparalleled in British drama."

The Daily Telegraph

The Scandi-gloom boom burgeoned here

Rarely has the British media so embarrassed itself as when it responded to one of the most important TV series of recent decades by banging on and on about the jumper worn by the character. The pensive Danes must think we are simpletons of the shallowest order. Still, enough Brits became hooked for the show to register as a phenomenon, pulling in more viewers than *Mad Men* despite those "difficult" subtitles and its atmospheric darkness, and opening up our sensibilities to the new wave of Scandinavian noir. *Wallander* had knocked at the door, *The Killing* pulled us into the shadows, and its successors then knew we'd follow them fiercely.

The precise procedural, spanning a complex murder mystery, political machinations and a grieving family (in Season One), had classic twists and red herrings, artful photography of Copenhagen and archly ambivalent acting. The breakout star was Sofie Gråbøl's detective Sarah Lund, an enigma even to herself with emotional disconnects and workaholic tendencies, which made "troubled" sleuths of previous generations seem blandly well-adjusted. Coverage swung between debate about her status as a feminist icon and cloying columns on the significance of that knitwear. Season Two maintained standards; the half-length third seemed an afterthought, and, of course, the US remake missed the mark.

If you liked this you'll like:
The Bridge, Wallander, Spiral.

THE TUDORS

CREATED BY:	Michael Hirst
STARRING:	Jonathan Rhys Meyers, Sam Neill, Henry Cavill, Natalie Dormer
DATES:	April 2007 – June 2010
SEASONS:	4
EPISODES:	38

SOUNDBITE:

"If I cannot please the King, will he kill me?"

Anne of Cleves

REVIEW:

"A primitively sensual period drama that critics could take or leave but viewers are eating up."

The New York Times

Passionate lovers fail to keep their heads

There had been films and series about Henry VIII and his six wives before, but none like this. Playing fast and loose with the historical facts, *The Tudors* (which despite its title examined the dynasty no further, Henry's story being a generous gift that keeps on giving) ramped up the sex and violence and charged into genuine psychological and erotic power. The performances were gutsy and convincing; the narrative, naturally, rattled royally along. Its premiere was the highest-rated on Showtime for three years.

Everyone knows the skeleton of the tale – impatient, selfish Henry flits from Catherine of Aragon through five more short-suffering queens while arguing with Cardinal Wolsey, Thomas More and Thomas Cromwell, defying the Pope and radically redrawing the map of British religion. Yet Hirst's version tosses away the school textbooks and goes for wild over worthy. The show looks gorgeous, and the life-and-death stakes faced by characters (Peter O'Toole, Max Von Sydow) add sweaty urgency. Pre-eminent among the passionate plots is the love and lust of Henry and Anne Boleyn. Natalie Dormer radiates charisma as proto-feminist Anne, defiant, bold: her teasing of Henry is almost tactile. And as Henry, Meyers (in a marathon portrayal of insecure egomania) is both slickly repellent and mournfully magnetic. For all his sins, Henry's ageing and physical decline is a picture of pathos. Thrilling television.

If you liked this you'll like:
The Borgias, Rome, Vikings.

MAD MEN

CREATED BY:	Matthew Weiner
STARRING:	Jon Hamm, Elisabeth Moss, Vincent Kartheiser, Christina Hendricks
DATES:	July 2007 – present
SEASONS:	7
EPISODES:	85 (ongoing)

SOUNDBITE:

"What you call love was invented by guys like me to sell nylons."

Don Draper

REVIEW:

"Stylized, visually arresting… an adult drama of introspection and the inconvenience of modernity in a man's world."

San Francisco Chronicle

Swinging with subtext under the stylish '60s surface

Mad Men is, on the gorgeous surface, a slow-burning drama about a prestigious 1960s Manhattan advertising agency, centring on its enigmatic lady-killer-in-chief Don Draper (Hamm). Yet Matthew Weiner has used that time and place to examine topical issues from an ingeniously skewed perspective. Sexism, racism, feminism, anti-semitism and marriage are all implicitly discussed through a harmonic haze of cigarette smoke and whisky breath. If *Mad Men* was a gift to style magazines – the clothes were a walking exhibition of lost elegance – its truth and lies cut deep.

As a tsunami of sweeping social changes and counter-cultural confusion hits the decade, Don and his peers – like the defiantly un-reconstructed Roger Sterling – lose their cocksure footing. Don's identity is in any case nebulous. The women – ambitious Peggy, stoic but ruthless Joan, increasingly bewildered Betty (the first Mrs Draper) and emblem of the new world Megan (the second Mrs Draper) – develop story arcs in which they bloom from cyphers to intricate individuals. Our sympathies switch as the times twitch like trigger-fingers. *Mad Men*, its tone always under-selling the sensational, has won even more awards than Sterling Cooper & Partners as it broodily covers the ground once covered by Updike and Roth. With layers and nuances that only a second or third viewing might reveal, *Mad Men* is hypnotic long-form television in excelsis.

If you liked this you'll like:
The Hour, Boss, Mildred Pierce.

CALIFORNICATION

CREATED BY:	Tom Kapinos
STARRING:	David Duchovny, Natasha McElhone, Evan Handler, Madeline Zima
DATES:	August 2007 – present
SEASONS:	7
EPISODES:	78

SOUNDBITE:

"I probably won't go down in history, but I will go down on your sister."

Hank

REVIEW:

"Male-fantasy sexism played for laughs… add pathos, L.A. entertainment industry sheen and a little Charles Bukowski and it all made sense. Sort of."

San Francisco Chronicle

The Sex Files

When David Duchovny announced he was going into treatment for sex addiction prior to Season Two screening, there were many who thought the show's end was nigh. We wouldn't be able to separate the actor from the character, they suggested: it wouldn't be funny when the show crossed lines of taboo any more. Well, *Californication* is nothing if not prepared to face things head on. Somehow, roguish charm outfought realism and conscience as Hank Moody's id continued to run amok for years, the boozy writer proving as implausibly irresistible to the women of the world as only fictitious characters penned by bullishly optimistic male writers can.

Few actors have scrambled their popular personas as wantonly as Duchovny does here, shifting from the subdued, enigmatic star of *The X-Files* to scandalous, self-loathing, priapic Hank, addicted to drink, drugs, bad decisions and career sabotage. Even his daughter Becca calls him a "poor man's Bukowski". Her long-suffering mother Karen (McElhone) flits between forgiveness and resolve, while Hank's agent and best friend Charlie (Handler) is no good influence. Still, lucrative offers fall Hank's way, only for him to recklessly blow them in pursuit of hedonism. The show's lingering tone was set by the pilot's opening scene, in which a nun performs fellatio on Hank in a church.

If you liked this you'll like:
Entourage, Hung, Masters Of Sex.

THE BIG BANG THEORY

CREATED BY:	Chuck Lorre, Bill Prady
STARRING:	Jim Parsons, Johnny Galecki, Kaley Cuoco, Kunal Nayyar, Simon Helberg
DATES:	September 2007 – present
SEASONS:	7 (Season 8 confirmed)
EPISODES:	159

SOUNDBITE:

"Sometimes your movements are so life-like I forget you're not a real boy."

Leonard to Sheldon

REVIEW:

"Bright and obvious as a cartoon yet written with a clean, precise patter of jokes. It's also very well cast."

People

Zingers + nerds x Sheldon = The Bazinga Equation

It's one of the great pop quiz curveballs that Chuck Lorre, the creator of *Two and a Half Men*, *Grace Under Fire*, *Dharma and Greg* and *The Big Bang Theory*, was a singer-guitarist in the 1980s and wrote the Deborah Harry hit "French Kissin' in the USA". After a shift writing for *Roseanne*, Lorre enjoyed a lucrative career move. The Charlie Sheen vehicle *Two and a Half Men* became America's highest-rated sitcom, and *The Big Bang Theory* has, in the several years since its launch, taken that title. Lorre's jokes may be of the predictable, plodding kind that leave a long pause while the cast wait for you to howl with laughter at their smart delivery, but it's clear the writer has honed a relaxed, populist formula.

Fundamentally a revenge-of-the-nerds fantasy, the show gives the viewer a gang of five: physicist room-mates Sheldon and Leonard, their equally geeky friends Howard and Raj, and the more streetwise, socially adept blonde waitress-actress across the hall, Penny. Brains versus beauty contrasts are emphasised between the boys' academic intellects and Penny's gumption and confidence. The show's neat juxtapositions of lust, microbiology and sci-fi references blends efficiently with skilful comic performances, particularly from the almost-Vulcan Parsons and the fast-reacting Cuoco.

If you liked this you'll like:
That 70s Show, Rules Of Engagement, My Name Is Earl.

TRUE BLOOD

CREATED BY:	Alan Ball
STARRING:	Anna Paquin, Stephen Moyer, Alexander Skarsgård, Sam Trammell
DATES:	September 2008 – 2014
SEASONS:	6
EPISODES:	70 (Season 7 imminent)

SOUNDBITE:

Sookie: "You're alive?"
Bill: "Technically, no."

REVIEW:

"Part mystery, part fantasy, part comedy, and all wildly imaginative exaggeration."

USA Today

Sookie meets bloodsuckers in not-so-deep South

Based on Charmaine Harris' novels *The Southern Vampire Mysteries*, *True Blood* was Alan Ball's curious choice of next project after *Six Feet Under*. Gothic, dealing with death? Yes. Smart and thoughtful? Less so. *True Blood*, after a promising first season, has become a frothy, sexy concoction, more of a guilty pleasure than anything of depth. It taps into the current vogue for all things vampiric with mad energy and relish, tossing into the mix werewolves, changelings, witches, faeries and great lashings of sex. It's not so much *Twilight* for grown-ups as *Twilight* with the repressed lust given full licence to come out and play. With dodgy Southern accents.

Sookie Stackhouse (Paquin) is a telepathic waitress (and "halfling") who falls in love with veteran gentleman vampire Bill (Moyer), but is soon also eyeing his more charismatic rival Eric (Skarsgård). Vampires are "out" in this world, drinking synthetic blood, and only feeding on humans if they're naughty. Much of the loopy plot involves itself with love triangles, but on its better days – its earlier seasons – *True Blood* touches on equal rights and discrimination against minorities (vampires) with some wit. There are some comic pops at religion and drug addiction too. Yet Ball has admitted its key motivation: "To me, vampires are sex, not abstinence. I'm 53. I don't care about high school students. I find them irritating and uninformed." Naysayers might argue that no TV character is as irritating as Sookie. *True Blood* pumps on into Season 7, its last.

If you liked this you'll like:
Buffy The Vampire Slayer, Game Of Thrones, The Vampire Diaries.

SONS OF ANARCHY

CREATED BY:	Kurt Sutter
STARRING:	Charlie Hunnam, Katey Sagal, Ron Perlman, Maggie Siff
DATES:	September 2008 – present
SEASONS:	6
EPISODES:	79 (Season 7 mooted, tbc)

SOUNDBITE:

"A true outlaw finds the balance between the passion in his heart and the reason in his mind. The outcome is the balance of might and right."

Jax Teller, reading his father's memoirs

REVIEW:

"A richly detailed portrait of self-righteous villainy."

Entertainment Weekly

Motorcycle boys ride on the wild side

Sons Of Anarchy has been the FX channel's highest-rated series ever, surpassing previous, equally unwholesome hits *The Shield*, *Nip/Tuck* and *Rescue Me*. The SOA are an outlaw motorcycle gang with many "charters", overseas as well as across the States. The charter we meet – SAMCRO – have their HQ in the fictional town of Charming, California, where they "protect" the area through intimidation, bribery and gun-running.

And yet, for the most part, the viewer roots for them. We get to know the personal, Shakespearean struggles of Jackson "Jax" Teller (the impressive Brit-export Hunnam), his lovers and family. His mother, Gemma (Sagal), is as ruthless as Boudicca; we alternately admire her strength and gasp at her manipulative evil. As the gang – all leather, tattoos and macho camaraderie on the surface, but hiding weak spots – come up against increasingly stubborn obstacles and inventive law enforcers, their bonds of loyalty are stretched to breaking point and betrayal.

Each series goes darker and deeper into its stories than you anticipate, burrowing in like a virus. With actors like Jimmy Smits and Drea de Matteo showing up in support, the show consistently ratchets up the sweaty, sinister suspense. As for Sagal – married to show-runner Sutter – is there an actor alive who's portrayed as many diversely unforgettable roles as Gemma, Peggy Bundy in *Married... With Children* and Leela in *Futurama*?

If you liked this you'll like:
Southland, True Detective, Rescue Me.

BREAKING BAD

CREATED BY:	Vince Gilligan
STARRING:	Bryan Cranston, Aaron Paul, Anna Gunn, Dean Norris
DATES:	January 2008 – September 2013
SEASONS:	5
EPISODES:	62

SOUNDBITE:

"I am not in danger, Skyler. I *am* the danger.
A guy opens his door and gets shot and
you think that of me? No. I am the one who
knocks."

Walter White

REVIEW:

"It's a drama that has chosen the slow burn
over the flashy explosion, and it's all the
hotter for that."

Time

Mr White turns to the dark side

Two years in the life of Walter White (Cranston) see him metamorphose from timid chemistry teacher with lung cancer and a midlife crisis to ruthless methamphetamine-cooking drug lord. At first, he sees this career switch as a means to leaving his family some money, but as his wild ride with sidekick Jesse Pinkman (Aaron Paul) lurches into increasingly dark scenarios he loses his moral compass. Bleak comedy becomes neo-realist opera.

Gilligan set out to turn "Mr. Chips into Scarface". Our sympathies darted back and forth as this unprecedented anti-hero defied predictability. Similarly, characters like his wife Skyler (Gunn) and brother-in-law Hank (Norris) wrestled with their consciences and became deeper embroiled in the maelstrom.

A surgical examination of free will and the lines between right and wrong, *Breaking Bad* used symbolism, suspense, Walt Whitman and a pink teddy bear to ramp up the tension, which in Seasons 2 and 3 grew close to unbearable. At first an internet and word-of-mouth hit rather than a runaway hype, the series was – despite eschewing most obvious cliff-hanger tropes - the ultimate in the "addictive" box-set experience, as fans found they constantly had to watch "just one more." Countless Emmy awards on, its finale was popular culture's most talked-about flourish of recent times. Nail-biting existentialism, doubling as a vice-like thriller.

If you liked this you'll like:
Mad Men, *The Sopranos*, *Weeds*.

MODERN FAMILY

CREATED BY:	Christopher Lloyd, Steven Levitan
STARRING:	Ed O'Neill, Sofía Vergara, Ty Burrell, Julie Bowen
DATES:	September 2009 – present
SEASONS:	5
EPISODES:	120 (Season 6 imminent)

SOUNDBITE:

"That's a library? I thought it was a church for a religion that didn't allow make-up."

Haley

REVIEW:

"Very, very funny, almost ruthlessly so… a master class in pace and brevity… prodigal in its zingers and snorters but austere in its construction."

The Atlantic

We've come a long, long way since The Waltons

Presented mockumentary style, with characters often acknowledging the camera, the most award-winning sitcom of recent years introduces us to three very different, though related, families in suburban L.A. There's Jay (O'Neill) and younger, glamorous Colombian wife Gloria (Vergara), Jay's daughter Claire (Bowen) and self-proclaimed "cool dad" Phil (Burrell), and Jay's lawyer son (Jesse Tyler Ferguson) and his partner Cameron (Eric Stonestreet). Each pairing has various children. The family tree matters less than the pitch-perfect jokes, acting, observations and charm: there is no weak link.

Ed O'Neill led another edgy family sitcom from 1987 to 1999, as grumpy, misanthropic patriarch Al Bundy in *Married…With Children*. Society's attitudes have changed since then, so O'Neill's dry presence resonates in this (much) more politically correct show with its nu-fangled multicultural relationships, adoption and same-sex marriage. Providing a career-making role for the va-va-voom Vergara, Bowen and Burrell, it also nods to US comedy's rich heritage with a recurring guest role for Shelley Long (Diane in *Cheers*) as Jay's ex-wife. As *USA Today* raved: "Not since *Frasier* has a sitcom offered such an ideal blend of heart and smarts, or proven itself so effortlessly adept at so many comic variations, from subtle wordplay to big-laugh slapstick to everything in between."

If you liked this you'll like:
Married…With Children, Arrested Development, Happy Endings.

THE GOOD WIFE

CREATED BY:	Robert King, Michelle King
STARRING:	Julianna Margulies, Josh Charles, Archie Panjabi, Alan Cumming, Christine Baranski
DATES:	September 2009 – present
SEASONS:	5
EPISODES:	112 (Season 6 confirmed)

SOUNDBITE:

"I've been hurt deeply. I imagine I will heal one day. But for now, we need a plan."

Alicia

REVIEW:

"A whip-smart blend of workplace derring-do and domestic melodrama, this series manages to stay both mainstream and offbeat… a neat trick."

Associated Press

The best box-set you've never heard of

The Good Wife has no obvious USP or gimmick, and rarely collects the column inches or web buzz of hipper, darker, HBO-style shows. Yet its consistency is its strength. *The Good Wife* is reliable. Not in a boring, plodding way, but in the sense that you feel safe in the hands of the writers and cast. You trust they won't insult your intelligence. The show is a sophisticated, sleek model of lean plots and classy acting. When they do blindside you with an emotional blow, you're not desensitised: it really hits.

Opening on the premise that Alicia Florrick (Margulies) has to return to work at a law firm when her politico husband (Chris Noth, *Sex and the City's* Mr Big) is jailed after a sex scandal, the show then fuses legal procedural with season-long story arcs which bring in love affairs, seething professional rivalries and moral dilemmas. Alicia's affair with Will (Charles) complicates matters, while the contributions of Kalinda (Panjabi), Diane (Baranski) and Eli (Cumming) serve as commentary on duplicity and diplomacy. *The Good Wife* probes money, power, courtroom brinkmanship and infidelity with an unflashy (if impeccably-dressed) rhythm and subtle subversion. Executive-produced by Ridley (and the late Tony) Scott, the show is as topical as it is elegant and empowering. Perhaps the sphinx-like Alicia is as close as we have to a female Don Draper?

If you liked this you'll like:
LA Law, Suits, Ally McBeal.

PARKS AND RECREATION

CREATED BY:	Greg Daniels, Michael Schur
STARRING:	Amy Poehler, Nick Offerman, Aziz Ansari, Rashida Jones, Chris Pratt, Aubrey Plaza
DATES:	April 2009 – present
SEASONS:	6
EPISODES:	112 (Season 7 confirmed)

SOUNDBITE:

"This is the hardest I've ever worked on anything since... wow, I've never worked hard on anything. What a cool life!"

Tom

REVIEW:

"It's family-friendly and adult-pleasing, over-the-top and nightmarish, witty and deep all at the same time."

Slant

The Office relocates to Pawnee, Indiana

Amy Poehler is a contender for the title of America's funniest woman. After departing *Saturday Night Live* after seven years Poehler's first vehicle as lead star was in *Parks And Recreation*. Daniels and Schur had been asked to come up with a spin-off of *The Office* (the US version), but "couldn't find the right fit". With Poehler signed up, they hit on the idea of an over-zealous, optimistic small-town government bureaucrat. What it does share with *The Office* is the mockumentary format and an element of cast improvisation. Early reactions to the first season were lukewarm, but after tweaks the show has developed into a cult favourite and a 2014 Golden Globe winner for Poehler – the year she was also co-hosting with Fey.

Poehler's idealistic Leslie Knope loves her home town Pawnee, Indiana with a passion, and dreams naively of becoming President of the USA. (Michelle Obama's guest cameo, then, is something of a coup). Leslie's best friend is Ann Perkins (Jones, a star of *The Office*), and colleagues include sarcastic, self-deluding Tom (Ansari), lovable slacker and Ann's ex Andy (Chris Pratt), cynical, bored April (Aubrey Plaza) and existentially subversive office director Ron Swanson (Offerman). Rob Lowe and Adam Scott join the team later, both knocking it out of the park with deft turns and loveable charm. It's Poehler's vehicle, but each of a crack comedy crew is adept at the wheel.

If you liked this you'll like:
The Office: An American Workplace, 30 Rock, Community.

GLEE

CREATED BY:	Ryan Murphy, Brad Falchuk, Ian Brennan
STARRING:	Lea Michele, Cory Monteith, Jane Lynch, Matthew Morrison
DATES:	May 2009 – present
SEASONS:	5
EPISODES:	107 (Season 6 confirmed as the last)

SOUNDBITE:

"I'd like your feedback as to whether I was brilliant or simply outstanding."

Rachel

REVIEW:

"When *Glee* works – which is often – it is transcendent, tear-jerking and thrilling like nothing else on TV."

Time

The TV equivalent of a sugar rush

By joining the all-singing, all-dancing, all-jazz-hands Glee Club, a group of high-school misfits escape their troubles and find acceptance and camaraderie, pursuing their dreams. Wait, come back!

What might, in less astute hands, have been old-fashioned cheesy schmaltz is given wings by arch-helmer Ryan Murphy's ear for whip-smart dialogue and sassy sarcasm. Barely a line in *Glee* doesn't contain a zinger, and when the wit is married to the buoyant performances and hearty singing of the cast, the sparky feel-good-isms of *Glee* are impossible to resist. The toughest cynic would struggle not to be swept along, especially as Murphy pre-empts scepticism by giving characters like Sue Sylvester (Lynch) the killer put-downs.

Glee is also so politically correct it hurts, with its disparate ensemble show-choir including every ethnicity and sexual persuasion and even a paraplegic guitarist. When Cory Monteith, the actor who'd played Finn, tragically died in 2013, the subsequent tribute episode "The Quarterback" was praised for its well-gauged sensitivity. As Rachel, Finn's on-off girlfriend, Lea Michele has proven to be the break-out star, her singing and acting throughout is quite dazzling. Ultimately, *Glee*, for all its impeccable social awareness and anti-bullying crusades, flourishes because the jokes are sharp, the songs are uplifting and it's a whole heap of poppy fun.

If you liked this you'll like:
Fame, Ugly Betty, Greek.

SOUTHLAND

CREATED BY:	Ann Biderman
STARRING:	Michael Cudlitz, Benjamin McKenzie, Regina King, Shawn Hatosy
DATES:	April 2009 – April 2013
SEASONS:	5
EPISODES:	43

SOUNDBITE:

"What do you think I am, the king of L.A.? I can't just make things disappear."

Officer Ben Sherman

REVIEW:

"*Southland* is commendably stinting and cold, a series that doesn't aim to please, and is all the more pleasurable for it."

The New York Times

Harrowing cop show which gets under your skin

Many cop shows are billed as "raw" and "authentic". Few have delivered on that promise as thoroughly as *Southland*, a series that never attracts the gushing of critics as much as other universally garlanded shows but also one that refuses to compromise in its pessimistic, compelling vision. It takes a harrowing look at contemporary Los Angeles and the angst felt by the LAPD officers who strain to keep the racial pressure cooker from blowing.

As much as it reveals streets meaner than a hell-on-earth, *Southland* is a study of character under duress. Officer John Cooper (Cudlitz) is secretly gay; Detective Lydia Adams (King) has to balance work with family; Detective Sammy Bryant (Hatosy) and Officer Ben Sherman (McKenzie) become a bonded but dysfunctional professional partnership. Whereas most cop shows spin around a case-of-the-week, *Southland* races through a catalogue of horrors, tragedies and bathos-laden misdemeanours. Nervy hand-held camerawork ratchets up the tension. We get right inside the gap between the officers' strengths and vulnerabilities. As it progresses, *Southland* becomes almost unremittingly depressing (a recommendation), with the leads facing ever more crushing daily blows, and questioning why they even try to clean up the city. A kind of "one that got away" among the classic twenty-first century US adult dramas, *Southland* deserves greater appreciation for its keen-eyed mix of energy and enervation.

If you liked this you'll like:
The Shield, True Detective, Breaking Bad.

BORGEN

CREATED BY:	Adam Price
STARRING:	Sidse Babett Knudsen, Birgitte Hjort Sørensen, Søren Malling, Emil Poulsen
DATES:	September 2010 – December 2013
SEASONS:	3
EPISODES:	30

SOUNDBITE:

"Management are discussing your meta-narrative."

Newsroom boss Alex, to previous newsroom boss Torben

REVIEW:

"A bleaker, Nordic version of *The West Wing*; it finds a remarkable amount of drama and suspense in centre-left alliances, pension plans and televised debates."

The New York Times

Walk-and-talk through the Danish corridors of power

So, were the Scandinavians a one-trick pony, masters of
the dark marathon murder mystery but turned to stone by
daylight? Far from it. The exquisite *Borgen* – arguably neck-
and-neck with *The Bridge* as the region's finest export yet
– might be, as *Newsweek* put it, "the best TV show you've
never seen". If you have, you'll know it's the only serious
contender to *The West Wing* as the most exhilarating show
made about politics and media-spin. Not one but two female
leads dominate, and we even learn a thing or two about the
compromises of coalition. Sounds a bit worthy? The show's
insights are leavened by lashings of stylish, sophisticated,
sexy soap and deft, droll performances.

Birgitte Nyborg (Knudsen), a centre-left moderate,
becomes the first female Danish prime minister, slightly
to her surprise. Her job requires considerable powers of
persuasion and endless tough decisions. Her marriage,
rock-solid at first, will suffer. In later seasons, she will fight
from different angles. Meanwhile, the media blow hot
and cold, not least ambitious, attractive TV news anchor
Katrine (Sørensen) and her colleagues. In Denmark, some
of the issues raised in the series' led to heated debates in
parliament. Elsewhere, the viewers just wanted – *needed* – to
know what happened next.

If you liked this you'll like:
The West Wing, The Bridge, Commander In Chief.

THE TRIP/ THE TRIP TO ITALY

CREATED BY:	Michael Winterbottom
STARRING:	Steve Coogan, Rob Brydon
DATES:	November 2010 and May 2014
SEASONS:	2
EPISODES:	12

SOUNDBITE:

Rob: "Where do you stand on Michael Bublé?"
Steve: "On his windpipe?"

REVIEW:

"On paper *The Trip* sounds like a cosy, luvvie, giant in-joke for Coogan and Brydon… but it is completely brilliant and hilarious."

The Scotsman

From Baker Street to the information superhighway...

"Sherlock is a triumph", wrote *The Independent*'s Tom Sutcliffe. "Witty and knowing, it understands that Holmes isn't really about plot but about charisma." Certainly the "Consulting Detective" with the astute logical reasoning has come a long way since Basil Rathbone's era. There were those who wondered why yet another Sherlock reinvention was afoot: the character is listed as "the most portrayed literary human character" by the *Guinness World Records*, with over seventy actors playing him in over 250 films. Yet Gatiss and Moffat, *Doctor Who* writing graduates, dreamed up this irreverent reboot of the sleuth, with Conan Doyle's man of mystery using modern technology (the internet, texting, GPS), to solve crimes. The show's inventive visuals added to the conjuring trick.

With John Watson – a doctor, recently returned from military service in Afghanistan – at first sceptical of this seemingly charmless man's abilities, he (like the viewer) needs to be convinced by his intellect and keen observations. Holmes becomes a celebrity (how modern), and conflicts ensue with arch-nemesis Moriarty (Andrew Scott). One of the briefest, but most perfectly formed, Series Two ends with the greatest cliffhanger of recent times. With Cumberbatch's rising star quality an added draw, Series Three became the UK's most popular drama for thirteen years.

If you liked this you'll like:
Elementary, Life On Mars, Jonathan Creek.

LUTHER

CREATED BY:	Neil Cross
STARRING:	Idris Elba, Ruth Wilson, Warren Brown, Dermot Crowley
DATES:	May 2010 – July 2013
SEASONS:	3
EPISODES:	14

SOUNDBITE:

DCI Luther: "You can revel in your brilliance for as long as you like Alice, but people slip up. Happens time and time again."

Alice Morgan: "Well that's just faulty logic postulated on imperfect data collection."

REVIEW:

"Gritty and ambiguous, *Luther* is captivating drama which delves into dark territory, bolstered by a powerhouse performance from Idris Elba."

Rotten Tomatoes

London as Gotham: Idris Elba scares up a storm

DCI John Luther (Elba) investigates serious crimes, and is a serious man. Obsessive about the job, passionate and sometimes a risk to those working or living with him, he pays a price for the darkness he confronts regularly. Alice (the charismatic Wilson), the murderer of the first episode, becomes a strange confidante, providing insight into the criminal mind. The scripts and taut performances grips the viewer in place from minute one; the intense vision of contemporary London leading to increasingly frightening scenarios. One episode had viewers checking under the bed afterwards before trying to sleep.

Those critics who baulked at the operatic use of cop-show tough-guy clichés missed the point. *Luther* wilfully amped up the tropes of wayward genius investigator, troubled personal life, insane criminals and moral ambiguity until they bled existential truth. This was police procedural as brainstormed by Paul Auster, Luke Rhinehart and Ken Russell. Equal parts stalked and intrigued by sociopathic Alice, inspired by David Bowie (the picture on the wall of Luther's grotty flat reveals so much about his psyche), Luther is a detective for people bored with detectives. Hungry for unbearably tense set pieces, he's the next level in modern crime's claustrophobic circles of hell. And let's face it: if Idris Elba ain't cool, nobody is.

If you liked this you'll like:
True Detective, The Fall, The Following.

DOWNTON ABBEY

CREATED BY:	Julian Fellowes
STARRING:	Hugh Bonneville, Elizabeth McGovern, Jim Carter, Michelle Dockery
DATES:	September 2010 — present
SEASONS:	4
EPISODES:	34 (Series 5 airs in 2014)

SOUNDBITE:

Matthew Crawley: "Mother, Lord Grantham has made the unwelcome discovery that his heir is a middle class lawyer, and the son of a middle class doctor."
Isobel Crawley: "*Upper* middle class!"

REVIEW:

"Melodrama is an uncool thing to trade in these days, but that's precisely why *Downton Abbey* is so pleasurable. The show is welcome counter-programming to the slow-burning despair and moral ambiguity of most quality drama on TV right now."

Vanity Fair

Britain's class divide = classy period drama

Beginning in the build-up to WWI, the all-conquering
Downton Abbey introduces the audience to the aristocratic
Crawley family and – below stairs – their servants. History's
great events – the war, the sinking of the *Titanic*, the Marconi
scandal, the formation of the Irish Free State – impact upon
their lives and on the class structure. The show has revived
the fortunes of the period drama, sweeping up global
accolades as the most successful British costume drama
since 1981's *Brideshead Revisited*.

Fellowes had won an Academy Award for writing the
Robert Altman film *Gosford Park* when first approached
for this, and was initially reluctant to cover similar ground.
The writer, a Conservative member of the House of Lords,
does not regret changing his mind. While the unconverted
deem the show "preposterous" – critic A.A. Gill has called it
"everything I despise and despair of on British television:
National Trust sentimentality, flogging an embarrassing,
demeaning and bogus vision of the place I live in" – other
commentators have applauded it as, "handsome, artfully
crafted and acted". Love stories flicker against repressed
urges. The death of a lead character (in the Christmas
Special 2012) upset and appalled the faithful. No matter:
the American audiences love it even more than the British,
and it's received more Emmy nominations than any non-US
show ever. The world is watching post-Edwardian Yorkshire.

If you liked this you'll like:
Brideshead Revisited, Upstairs Downstairs, Parade's End.

BOARDWALK EMPIRE

CREATED BY:	Terence Winter
STARRING:	Steve Buscemi, Michael Pitt, Michael Shannon, Kelly Macdonald, Stephen Graham
DATES:	September 2010 — November 2014
SEASONS:	5
EPISODES:	60

SOUNDBITE:

"You can't be half a gangster, Nucky. Not any more."

Jimmy Darmody

REVIEW:

"An expensive, explicit, character-driven program, tackling material no broadcast network or movie studio would dare touch."

Variety

Fear and loathing in Atlantic City

The show which gave HBO back its crown as the king of serial US drama. *Boardwalk Empire* opened in a blaze of hype – it's costly, extended pilot was directed (with no expense spared) by Martin Scorsese and written by *The Sopranos* alumnus, Terence Winter. Yet it wasn't until it dropped the flash-bang and settled into its groove that its true merits became evident. The show is a master-class in multiple-strand storytelling.

Which isn't to say it shirks on the provocation – violence and sex are rarely far away. Set in Atlantic City, New Jersey, during the Prohibition-era, it stars the ever-watchable Buscemi as Nucky Thompson, a corrupt politician who controls the city. Nucky charms (or wheedles) allies and adversaries from the mob and the government as his bootlegging activities come under scrutiny as well as against equally ruthless competition. Around him circle ambivalent prodigy Jimmy (Michael Pitt), his pained wife Margaret (Macdonald), his envious brother Eli (Shea Whigham) and an ambitious young Al Capone (Graham).

The classic put-upon artful dodger who the audience know is evil but can't help half-hoping will duck his comeuppance, Nucky is just one powerful character in a show loaded with powerful characters. The cinematography throughout is beautiful, and these tales of broken love, misguided loyalty and foolhardy betrayal get under your skin, aiding all five series' build inexorably to a punishing, powerful pay-off.

If you liked this you'll like:
The Sopranos, Magic City, Fargo.

THE WALKING DEAD

DEVELOPED BY: Frank Darabont

STARRING: Andrew Lincoln, Steven Yeun, Norman Reedus, Lauren Cohan

DATES: October 2010 – present

SEASONS: 4

EPISODES: 51 (Season 5 to air in 2014)

SOUNDBITE:

"I had to keep hope alive, didn't I?"

Rick Grimes

REVIEW:

"Consistently thrilling, with solid character development and enough gore to please grindhouse fans."

Rotten Tomatoes

The zombie chiller it's OK to like...

Rick Grimes (Lincoln), a Sheriff's deputy, has been in a coma for weeks, after being shot on duty. He awakes to find that the world has been overrun by zombies, and he's the only human left alive… it seems. Heading off in search of his family, Rick realizes he is wide-awake in a living nightmare, with scores of zombies giving him a chilling welcome everywhere he goes. Encountering a group of tough and resilient survivors, Rick and the gang must do what they can to fend off the hungry zombie hordes while ruthlessly competing with other diehard humans in order to live.

Frank Darabont, best-known for his film adaptations of Stephen King novels *The Shawshank Redemption* and *The Green Mile*, executive-produces this surprise success story that was based on an original comic book series. A history of scripting horror trash like *A Nightmare On Elm Street III* probably helped him nail it. *The Walking Dead* has grown in gravitas while making its grizzly path to popularity: Season Four's premiere attracted over 16 million viewers – the most-watched telecast in basic cable history.

In its bleak, washed-out, dog-eat-dog world, Andrew Lincoln (once Egg in *This Life*) has redefined his quintessentially British image and tackled the lead character's personal, and literal, demons – sometimes sudden, sometimes simmering – with unexpected aplomb.

If you liked this you'll like:
Dexter, Being Human, In The Flesh.

GAME OF THRONES

CREATED BY:	David Benioff, D.B. Weiss
STARRING:	Peter Dinklage, Lena Headey, Kit Harington, Nikolaj Coster-Waldau, Charles Dance, Emilia Clarke
DATES:	April 2011 – present
SEASONS:	4 (Seasons 5 and 6 confirmed)
EPISODES:	39

SOUNDBITE:

"When you play the game of thrones, you win or you die. There is no middle ground."

Cersei Lannister

REVIEW:

"A dizzying array of characters, splendid performances and a scope and grandeur like nothing else on television."

Variety

One of the world's biggest shows: it will go on

Swords and sorcery, boobs and beheadings – *Game of Thrones* has critics drooling (in a good way) and has been described as "*The Sopranos* in Middle Earth". Based on George R.R. Martin's lengthy series of fantasy novels, the show's already guaranteed two more seasons and given its rabid fanbase will doubtless play on long beyond that.

Set across sprawling fictional landscapes, the show's skill lies in interweaving multiple storylines and taking its time about it. It luxuriates in droll dialogue while keeping addicted viewers perked up with startling, sudden scenes of violence, nudity and flying CGI dragons. It explores family, religion, superstition, trust, lust, betrayal, and man's (and woman's) craving for power. Its greatest trick has often been to misdirect: just as the audience believe one character or clan is being set up as the central base, the ground opens up beneath their feet, and ours, with a grandstanding twist. There is much Machiavellian manipulation and machination as various pretenders to the iron throne crawl closer to the ultimate face-off.

If pomposity ever threatens to set in, Peter Dinklage's brilliantly executed Tyrion Lannister is there to offer irreverence and cunning. And if one plotline is stalling, don't worry, there are countless others ready to pick up any slack. The seasons usually climax in an epic battle or a shock killing, but after all the "sexposition" the put-upon characters have had to endure, it's good for them, and us, to blow off a little steam…

If you liked this you'll like:
The Borgias, The Tudors, Camelot.

THE BRIDGE

CREATED BY:	Hans Rosenfeldt
STARRING:	Sofia Helin, Kim Bodnia, Puk Scharbau, Dag Malmberg
DATES:	September 2011 – present
SEASONS:	2 (Season 3 confirmed for 2015)
EPISODES:	20

SOUNDBITE:

"The most important task is to protect your colleague. Let me make this clear: I am your colleague."

Martin to Saga

REVIEW:

"When it comes to putting clever, kick-ass women with challenging social skills at the centre of the story, Scandinavia has it covered."

The Guardian

A crossover hit with multiple personalities

Despite the prominence of *The Killing*'s Sarah Lund and Stieg Larsson's Lisbeth Salander, there was still an appetite for a maverick Scandinavian female lead with both temperamental issues and indomitable drive. Though *The Killing* got the column inches, *The Bridge*'s sustained peaks of perfection outclassed it. The show benefited from the best mismatched-couple cop-buddies act of the twenty-first century. The evolving rapport of Saga (Helin) and Martin (Bodnia) offered pathos and dry humour; the plot presented social comment and suspense.

A body is found on the Oresund Bridge between Sweden and Denmark, placed precisely on the border. Malmo cop Saga and Copenhagen cop Martin must share jurisdiction. They are very different people. Martin has his own demons but is convention personified when placed next to charismatic loner Saga, who cannot relate to people and (it is popularly assumed) has Asperger's syndrome. Their trust develops (with glitches, of course) as they pursue killers, terrorists and scientists. Sub-plots and secondary characters multiply with each episode.

Like the Choir Of Young Believers' theme song, "Hollow Talk", Helin and Bodnia are brittle but resonant. *The Bridge* is Nordic in that it looks icily sublime and explores demands for reform and justice, but its charisma and cynical charm, avoiding genre cliché, attain universal truths. In a shock twist, both a Franco-British remake, *The Tunnel*, and a US one are halfway decent.

If you liked this you'll like:
Salamander, Hinterland, The Tunnel.

HOMELAND

DEVELOPED BY: Howard Gordon, Alex Gansa

STARRING: Claire Danes, Damian Lewis, Mandy Patinkin, Morena Baccarin

DATES: October 2011 – present

SEASONS: 3

EPISODES: 36 (Season 4 to air in 2014)

SOUNDBITE:

"Something's going on. None of this makes sense."

Carrie

REVIEW:

"*Homeland* is one of the rare spy dramas where the personal stories feel germane to the plot, not just an insert."

USA Today

Spy Hard: Carrie (eventually) loses the plot

Homeland emerged as a tense, twitchy, paranoid espionage drama driven by a compelling, award-grabbing performance from Claire Danes as Carrie Mathison, a CIA agent with massive insight but a mountain of personal issues. Adapted by graduates of *24* from an original Israeli series (*Prisoners Of War*), its clever premise saw American Marine and ex-POW Nicholas Brody (Lewis) return from Iraq to a hero's welcome while Carrie suspects he's been "turned" by the enemy.

With sharp characterisation, unseen twists and a voyeuristic interest in both leads' personal lives, *Homeland* – beloved by Barack Obama – was exciting and engaging for its first, excellent season. It did not sugar-coat the USA's methods of gathering intelligence. Once the trump card of Brody's innocence/guilt was upturned, the second stuttered, unsure where to go. The third, with Lewis often absent and Danes now over-acting wildly and bizarrely to distract us from the increasing ludicrousness of the plot, was nothing short of a flailing debacle, ripe for parody and offering unintended laughs. Yet *Homeland* retains enough goodwill that diehards hope the fourth season will rediscover the old magic. It needs to uncover new intelligence.

If you liked this you'll like:
Spooks, 24, Tinker Tailor Soldier Spy.

BOSS

CREATED BY:	Farhad Safinia
STARRING:	Kelsey Grammer, Connie Nielsen, Kathleen Robertson, Martin Donovan
DATES:	October 2011 – October 2012
SEASONS:	2
EPISODES:	18

SOUNDBITE:

"There are tanks in the streets. How did we get here, to this fractured place?"

Mayor Tom Kane

REVIEW:

"A wholly impressive drama that comes out of the gate with gravitas, swagger, originality and intrigue… has the potential to become a game-changer."

Hollywood Reporter

Frasier Crane does Citizen Kane

One of the great injustices of recent TV years was the cancellation of *Boss* after just two seasons, a victim of disappointing viewing figures and the vagaries of its network, Starz. The US premium cable channel hoped for *Boss* to do for it what *The Sopranos* had done for HBO, *Dexter* for Showtime, *The Shield* for FX or *Mad Men* for AMC. Ultimately, those ambitions were unrealistic – *Boss* is no crowd-pleaser. However, the series left its mark with unremittingly dark, dramatic storylines and a view of the crossover between the political and the personal which made *House Of Cards'* Frank Underwood's ego seem moderately-sized.

There's something about actors once known for sitcoms – Bryan Cranston, Woody Harrelson – getting grimy. Here, Grammer (lovable over-educated windbag in *Frasier*) is astonishingly credible as an amoral King Lear. Mayor of Chicago, his Tom Kane is diagnosed with a degenerative dementia disorder. He largely keeps this secret as he tightly holds on to his power. Kane's sham marriage to Meredith (the regal Nielsen), his relationship with his drug-addict daughter and twisted rapport with his closest advisers and rivals can only suffer. The bad karma spirals in a miasma of sex, lies, spin and delusions of immortality. Shot with washed-out yet lecherous originality (Gus Van Sant directed the pilot), *Boss* is the big, bruising one that got away.

If you liked this you'll like:
Breaking Bad, House Of Cards, The Borgias.

THE RETURNED

CREATED BY:	Fabrice Gobert
STARRING:	Anne Cosigny, Frédéric Pierrot, Clotilde Hesme, Céline Sallette
DATES:	November 2012 – present
SEASONS:	1 (Season 2 confirmed)
EPISODES:	8

SOUNDBITE:

"What you're about to see transcends any kind of logic, and changes the way we see the world."

Pierre

REVIEW:

"Although the first episode is mostly a triumph of mood and underplayed emotion, there are signs that the plot will twist itself into more gothic knots…"

The Independent

The French do the Undead

A simmering, shadowy supernatural drama based on the 2004 film *They Came Back* (*Les Revenants*), this artful, elegiac French slow-burner was the first subtitled series on Channel 4 for over two decades. It won the International Emmy for Best Drama Series, won fans from Stephen King to *Liberation* (who lazily compared it to David Lynch), and proved that gently worrying our imaginations is much scarier than generic schlock-horror tactics. It's perhaps the thinking-too-much person's *The Walking Dead*. Scottish post-rock band Mogwai's score is suitably sensitive yet sinister.

In a small French village in the Alps, a coach full of schoolchildren plummets off a road into the valley. Mourning ensues. But then we see one of the kids walking in the mountains, confused, not knowing she's dead. Several more dead now reappear in town… a suicidal bridegroom, a small boy, a serial killer. They try to pick up their old lives, as strange, subtle phenomena occur and unexplained markings appear on the bodies of both the living and the dead. Grief becomes hope or frightened bewilderment. Old lovers try to see the positives in the creepiness; the religious ponder a power-grab. Something bigger will take control… it's like a zombie apocalypse directed by Andrei Tarkovsky at his most poetic.

If you liked this you'll like:
Broadchurch, American Gothic, In The Flesh.

AMERICAN HORROR STORY

CREATED BY:	Ryan Murphy, Brad Falchuk
STARRING:	Jessica Lange, Evan Peters, Frances Conroy, Sarah Paulson
DATES:	October 2011 – present
SEASONS:	3
EPISODES:	38 (Season 4 to air in 2014)

SOUNDBITE:

"No matter how gruesome or horrible the murder, you can always find someone who'll buy the house."

Marcy

REVIEW:

"So far over the top that the top is a microscopic speck in its rear-view mirror."

HitFix

A nightmare in waiting. You have been warned.

Surely Ryan Murphy had worked out all his curious kinks in *Nip/Tuck* and, with the runaway success of *Glee*, was now a family-friendly show-runner? Not so. With this macabre creation he threw himself – and us – into a writhing snake-pit of clammy night terrors. Cleverly, *American Horror Story* conceives each season as a self-contained story with its own characters and locations, meaning it can wrap up and shock afresh each time. Cast members do reappear though, most notably the revitalised and estimable Jessica Lange, pocketing Emmys and Golden Globes while having a ball channelling Joan Crawford and Elsa Lanchester.

The first season, *Murder House*, deals with infidelity and depression in a haunted house setting. The second, *Asylum,* goes into an institution for the insane, where there's sadism and demonic possession. *Coven* gives us witches and voodoo, while the forthcoming fourth season – *Freak Show* – promises a carnival of skin-crawling yuckiness. Riddled with screams, gore, "mashed faces and dead babies", *American Horror Story* is not for the faint-hearted, and Murphy (with frequent collaborator, Falchuk) tend to see overcooking things as their job description. Knowingly outrageous, their lurid vision is both camp and claustrophobic, but you feel the characters' fears and – perhaps unfortunately – take them with you. *American Horror Story*: You may not want to watch it, but you can't dare look away.

If you liked this you'll like:
Hannibal, Penny Dreadful, Carnivale.

NASHVILLE

CREATED BY:	Callie Khouri
STARRING:	Connie Britton, Hayden Panettiere, Clare Bowen, Charles Esten
DATES:	October 2012 – present
SEASONS:	2
EPISODES:	43 (Season 3 to air in 2014)

SOUNDBITE:

"Turns out hooking up with a married man isn't the worst thing you can do…"

Juliette Barnes

REVIEW:

"The recipe may go back to your grandma or beyond, but that doesn't mean you won't eat two helpings and beg for more."

Miami Herald

C&W music made flesh: good honest soapy froth

Beginning as a kind of Country and Western cover version of *A Star Is Born* or *All About Eve* (established star threatened by up-and-coming starlet), *Nashville* soon found its natural shape as a soapy, frothy, wonderfully absurd fountain of well-soundtracked camp. Rarely has the world of C&W seemed so glamorously melodramatic and incident-packed. If Robert Altman's film of the same name set in a similar milieu was packed with small truths, Khouri's creation is overstuffed with magnificently silly plot twists.

Khouri was previously best known for the 1992 movie *Thelma and Louise*, but if that film was a feminist milestone, *Nashville* at first sets its female leads warring against each other in the cut-throat world of the music biz. As established "Queen of Country" Rayna James (Britton)'s career falters, younger and "sexier" pop star Juliette Barnes (Panettiere) emerges as pretender to the throne. To complicate matters, they fight over men. *Nashville* swiftly realizes it needs to cast its net wider, so the spot-lit pair begrudgingly form a tolerant relationship of sorts, as around them couples form and split and managers and record labels grow increasingly soulless in the name of capitalism. Take none of this seriously (the cast don't: Panettiere's diva antics are a joy to behold) and the show is a sugary, glamorous, addictive fun-fest. "Does the drama never end?" stage-sighs Rayna. Storming songs and performances are a bonus.

If you liked this you'll like:
Revenge, Scandal, Dallas.

THE NEWSROOM

CREATED BY:	Aaron Sorkin
STARRING:	Jeff Daniels, Emily Mortimer, Olivia Munn, Sam Waterston
DATES:	June 2012 – present
SEASONS:	2 (Season 3 to air 2014)
EPISODES:	19

SOUNDBITE:

"Except for the things we did wrong, we did everything right."

Will McAvoy

REVIEW:

"At its best it has wit, sophistication and manic energy. At its worst, the show chokes on its own sanctimony."

The New York Times

Compulsory viewing for fans of The West Wing

Sorkin's trademark rapid-fire dialogue and grandstanding monologues had won copious compliments with *The West Wing* and *The Social Network,* but his behind-the-scenes look at a TV studio in *Studio 60 On The Sunset Strip* went – according to *Time* magazine –"from buzz to bust". Sorkin was now, reckoned the backlash, putting lessons before laughs, pontification before propulsion. Many similar jibes were pitched at *The Newsroom,* which replaced the White House and Studio 60 with a cable news channel. Behind these scenes, the idealistic staff – hamstrung by crushes and love triangles – strived to produce a news show while overcoming corporate and commercial dictates.

At Atlantic Cable News, maverick anchorman Will McAvoy (Daniels) and improbably-named executive-producer MacKenzie McHale (Mortimer), bicker and flirt like sharp-witted off-cuts from a screwball comedy. As do pairings among their underlings, while the likes of Jane Fonda, Hope Davis and Marcia Gay Harden offer rich cameos. Usually, the cast beat their comedic demons in time to do the right, decent thing, at least in left-wing liberal terms. Applying the same shades to reporters as Sorkin did to politicians in *The West Wing* – rendering characters usually portrayed as "Machiavellian or dumb" as "romantic, swashbuckling, optimistic"– *The Newsroom* gets wiser, sharper and funnier as it settles in, and is intellectually astute enough to revel in irony; but its battle against cynicism is what makes it a righteous joy.

If you liked this you'll like:
The West Wing, Studio 60 On The Sunset Strip, 30 Rock.

GIRLS

CREATED BY:	Lena Dunham
STARRING:	Lena Dunham, Allison Williams, Jemima Kirke, Zosia Mamet
DATES:	April 2012 – present
SEASONS:	3
EPISODES:	32 (Season 4 to air 2014)

SOUNDBITE:

"Am I seriously the only one of us who prides herself on being a truly authentic person?"

Hannah

REVIEW:

"Raw, audacious, nuanced and richly, often excruciatingly funny."

Time

Zeitgeist-grasping comedy of failure

Lena Dunham's second film, *Tiny Furniture*, caught the eye of US comedy mogul Judd Apatow (executive-producer of *Girls*), who declared that an HBO show from her would offer "realistic females". Much of *Girls* is based on Dunham's own experiences. Her Hannah, an aspiring writer, is told by her parents they'll no longer financially support her as they have since she graduated, and she's left to fend for herself amid the trendy vintage stores of Brooklyn. She and her circle of friends navigate their twenties "one mistake at a time".

Girls has often been termed the anti-*Sex and the City*, but Dunham says she revered that show "as much as any girl of my generation". But these girls – twenty-first century slackers who'd never use the word "slackers" – don't have the moneyed lifestyles of Carrie and co. They're forced to downsize their over-educated dreams to fit a reality of transient jobs and even more transient relationships. While the show has been slammed by detractors for a shallow fixation with social media, STDs and narcissistic self-dramatisation (as well as its "whiteness") its fans have acclaimed its bleak candour. *Hollywood Reporter* hailed its depiction of "real female friendships, the angst of emerging adulthood, sexuality, self-esteem, body image, intimacy in a tech-savvy world that promotes distance… all laced together with humour and poignancy".

If you liked this you'll like:
The Mindy Project, Don't Trust The B---- In Apartment 23, Awkward.

HOUSE OF CARDS

CREATED BY:	Beau Willimon
STARRING:	Kevin Spacey, Robin Wright, Kate Mara, Corey Stoll
DATES:	February 2013 – present
SEASONS:	2
EPISODES:	26 (Season 3 to air 2015)

SOUNDBITE:

"A great man once said, everything is about sex. Except sex. Sex is about power."

Frank Underwood

REVIEW:

"Deeply cynical about human beings as well as politics, and almost gleeful in its portrayal of limitless ambition."

The Denver Post

Spacey brings Richard III to Washington DC

It seems faintly implausible that *House of Cards* was based on a 1990 British thriller, as if *Deadwood* was based on a Wendy Craig sitcom, yet such is the case. The show reveals countless more trump cards up its sleeve however as, fuelled by a performance of clinical malice by the peerless Spacey (returning to the kind of oily, sinister-charming role he does best), it wipes the table. Released by Netflix on its streaming service with all the first season available at once, the show recognised our tendency to "binge-watch" and pioneered a new business-production model. It seems indisputable that streaming is the way forward now.

Few themes can turbo-charge a drama as well as betrayal and revenge, and *House Of Cards* is knowingly Shakespearean (*Othello*, *Richard III*) in its ramping-up of envy and moral turpitude. The premise sees Spacey's Washington-based Democrat (and House majority whip) scheme and manipulate to get back at those who passed him over for Secretary Of State. Robin Wright plays his Lady Macbeth; Kate Mara the reporter and lover in whom he confides (at first). With David Fincher producing (and directing the opening two episodes), what might be hokum in lesser hands tightens into a hypnotic examination of a modern-day Machiavelli. "Working in film doesn't allow for complex characterisations the way television does," remarked Fincher. As for Willimon, the show's creator, he has served as an aide to Hillary Clinton and Governor Howard Dean.

If you liked this you'll like:
Boss, The West Wing, Borgen.

BROADCHURCH

CREATED BY:	Chris Chibnall
STARRING:	David Tennant, Olivia Colman, Jodie Whittaker, David Bradley
DATES:	March 2013 – present
SEASONS:	1
EPISODES:	8 (Season 2 confirmed for 2015)

SOUNDBITE:

"This house, this town, this job of mine: it's all I'm ever gonna be, innit? I know every second of it, and every second of it to come."

Mark Latimer

REVIEW:

"Manages to be both a finely crafted piece of suspenseful entertainment and an emotionally resonant examination of grief, loss and moral confusion."

Huffington Post

The most acclaimed UK crime story in years

Broadchurch won Baftas as Best Drama Series and for actors Colman (who seems to be the new Judi Dench of awards) and *Our Friends In The North* veteran David Bradley. Something of a word-of-mouth hit, its TV audience grew and grew as more caught on and caught up. An American remake called *Gracepoint* is on the way, with David Tennant again cast as the lead detective.

Many noted some similarity with *The Killing*, but in fact the script predated the brilliantly gloomy Danish show by several years. Chibnall's background was in *Doctor Who* and *Torchwood*, but this offered a refreshingly different, far more subtle role for Tennant. An ensemble drama exploring the ways in which a death affects a community in the Dorset region, it stitched strands of poetry and pathos into a compulsive whodunnit. When the seaside town of Broadchurch is rocked by the murder of an 11-year-old boy, Tennant's DI Hardy is hired to head the investigation, a decision resented by DS Miller (Colman), who knows the area and family involved. An insistent media frenzy doesn't help matters. The boy's father (Andrew Buchan) becomes an immediate suspect, but every viewer will form their own theories…

If you liked this you'll like:
Top Of The Lake, Happy Valley, Southcliffe.

ORANGE IS THE NEW BLACK

CREATED BY:	Jenji Kohan
STARRING:	Taylor Schilling, Laura Prepon, Kate Mulgrew, Danielle Brooks
DATES:	July 2013 – present
SEASONS:	2
EPISODES:	26 (Season 3 confirmed for 2015)

SOUNDBITE:

Piper: "She's a weird girl."
Poussey: "Yeah, 'you gonna die' is really vague. Like totally open for interpretation."

REVIEW:

"Netflix finally achieves its eureka moment with a terrifically entertaining programme that's truly and bracingly original."

TV Guide

The future's orange: this jailhouse rocks

Thirty-something, upper-middle-class bisexual blonde Piper Chapman (Schilling) is more than a little thrown when she's jailed for helping ex-girlfriend Alex (Prepon) carry drug money ten years previously. So is her fiancé. In prison she has a lot to learn fast, finding a niche in the social hierarchy and redrawing her relationship with Alex. As the *Washington Post* remarked of the new show from the *Weeds* creator: "In this magnificent and thoroughly engrossing series, prison is still the pits. But it is also filled with the entire range of human emotion and stories, all of which are brought vividly to life in a world where a stick of gum could ignite either a romance or a death threat."

Based on Piper Kerman's memoir of her year in a women's jail, the show gave new-kid-on-the-block Netflix an even bigger hit than *House Of Cards*, and has basked in plaudits for its sense of character and multi-cultural authenticity, as well as Kohan's trademark jet-black humour. Laverne Cox, as Sophia Burset, has been lionised as the first transgender woman to play a high-profile transgender character. Unpredictable, salty, madcap but focussed, *Orange*… makes its serious points sting and its sassy-scary stories sing with an acute perception of culture-clashes. As you'll discover, every inmate is an intrigue…

If you liked this you'll like:
Weeds, Six Feet Under, Oz.

TRUE DETECTIVE

CREATED BY:	Nic Pizzolatto
STARRING:	Matthew McConaughey, Woody Harrelson, Michelle Monaghan
DATES:	January 2014 – present
SEASONS:	1 (Season 2 confirmed for 2015)
EPISODES:	8

SOUNDBITE:

"There's a feeling – you might notice it sometimes – this feeling like life has slipped through your fingers, like the future is behind you, like it's always been behind you…"

Marty

REVIEW:

"Performances by Harrelson and McConaughey reel the viewer in, while the style, vision and direction make it hard to turn away."

Rotten Tomatoes

The most acclaimed show since The Wire...

The most watched first season in HBO's history, overtaking *The Sopranos* and *Game Of Thrones*, *True Detective* is to continue in an anthology format, with each series featuring a different cast and story. It remains to be seen if the liberally lauded, southern gothic opener can be surpassed. Boasting two experienced, previously taken-for-granted actors in devastating, dirty form, the series drew universal acclaim. In fact, so breathlessly eulogised was *True Detective* that the normally dignified, above-the-fray *The Good Wife* snuck in a parody of it. The show made great use of its South Louisiana locations and was fearless in allowing scenes of long meaningful silences to say as much as Pizzolatto's evocative dialogue.

The lives of detectives Rustin Cohle (McConaughey) and Marty Hart (Harrelson) grow entangled over seventeen years in pursuit of a serial killer. Both have personal demons of their own. The audience enters during the present day, then the timeline shifts and flits through their past, crossing corruption, oil pollution and religious zealots. Director Cary Joji Fukunaga's resonant backdrops and Pizzolatto's eerie fusion of pulp, nihilism, literary allusion and creepy supernatural horror encourage the story to take its time, pitching noir against light, ranging from soliloquys to nuance. As the *L.A. Times* put it, "slow and steady without ever seeming to drag... even the briefest scenes seem to imply life beyond the frame..." The rumours of A-list Hollywood stars lining up for Season Two have begun...

If you liked this you'll like:
Boss, Ray Donovan, Twin Peaks.

FARGO

CREATED BY:	Noah Hawley
STARRING:	Billy Bob Thornton, Martin Freeman, Allison Tolman, Colin Hanks
DATES:	April 2014 – present
SEASONS:	1
EPISODES:	10

SOUNDBITE:

Postal worker: "This is highly irregular."
Lorne Malvo: "No. Highly irregular is the time I found a human foot in a toaster oven. This is just odd."

REVIEW:

"FX's *Fargo* is like what you might get if you asked someone who hadn't seen the Coen brothers' Oscar-winning film in years to describe it: the small-town quirkiness, the Minnesota accents, the stoic bad guys and, of course, the blood."

Time Out Chicago